design focus Media Students Work of John Maeda

# ACG

M.I.T. Media Laboratory Aesthetics & Computation Group

设计新视点丛书 麻省理工学院媒体实验室

# 约翰·梅达的学生作品

mit media laboratory

aesthetics + computation group

## 麻省理工学院

### 回顾

一九八零年媒体实验室的轮廓由尼古拉斯·尼格罗邦特与杰罗米·维斯乐初步奠定，之后由建筑机械集团发展壮大，并建立在该实验室教师的开创性工作上，如：在概念上的马维·明斯基，学术上的西蒙·帕比特，音乐上的巴里·维可，平面设计方面的穆里尔·库朋，影视方面的安德列·利曼，全息摄影方面的史蒂芬·班顿。一九八五年十月一日，在新设计的贝聿铭物业名为维斯乐的大厦里，实验室正式对外开业。

在实验室成立的第一个十年里，其实验室活动大多数集中在传统实物图像的抽象电子内容，有助于创造当今流行的领域，如数码影视及多媒体。

这种计划成功地引向了正被日益关注的比特如何与原子相遇的问题：即电子信息如何与日常物体重叠。实验室在学术与工业合作上走在前面，它没有依照传统的分门别类，而是提供独特的环境来探索基础的研究与应用。

### 学术计划

与麻省理工学院的其他实验室不同的是，媒体实验室包括学位研究课程及研究项目。实验室的教师与高级研究员约三十人，另外有八十名职员为实验室的研究，设施及管理工作提供协助。在读研究生共一百六十四人，硕士生与博士生几乎各占一半，其中一百三十八人就读媒体艺术和科学课程，其余二十六人在麻省理工学院的其他科系就读，但在媒体实验室的指导下进行研究工作。另外，约一百五十名大学生每年通过麻省理工学院的“研究生研究机会计划”来实验室工作。

### 研究协会

目前三个主要的研究协会承担了实验室的大部分工作，协会基金由企业赞助商提供。协会的许多技术及软件通过麻省理工学院的实验进行测试及提炼，并与个别的会员公司合作。

“数据生活”协会处理比特与人之间的内部联系，还有在线领域的事情，研究着重以下四个方面：媒体／演示定义声音和画面的结构图像，将网络与娱乐相结合，逐步形成叙述故事的观念。行动／相互作用探索言语、手势及情感，还有令人投入的交流环境。儿童／文化包括学习、建造、设计，以及儿童与各个年龄段的成年人在各方面的合作。“联系／社区”建立合作、探索、设计以及随意的全球性互动环境。

"未来新闻研究协会"为麻省理工学院媒体实验室和成员公司提供探索及开发关于提高新闻收集与传播的技术论坛，其目的是提高制作效率，随时传送，便于展示，加强编辑、广告内容与消费者之间的关系。"未来新闻研究协会"侧重四个方面的研究：由电脑提供及为电脑制作的新闻描述；消费者行为的观察及模仿；展示与互动设计；还有应用。该协会为数据管理开发技术，在新闻提供者与观者之间搭起桥梁，以新的手段表现新闻内容。

"智能协会"于一九九五年十月在媒体实验室建成十周年庆典上正式宣布成立。该协会探索超越常规领域的移动电脑形式，如PC机或携带式电脑，通过添加智能功能使原产品变为全新或另一种产品。普通产品如烤面包机、门锁拉手或鞋，通过了解其用者的习惯及感受而解决问题。通过对事物的敏感与周到的考虑，使信息技术加强我们日常生活的质量。"智能协会"把出色的跨学科人才集中在一起，在实验室与其赞助机构之间建起紧密的研究合作关系。

## 特别兴趣小组

实验室成立了一批规模较小、专注于特别兴趣的小组，这些小组处理特别的课题。现已有六个小组正在运作或还在组建中：

"明日玩具"小组，探索数据革命改变玩具和娱乐世界的途径。

PENNY PC小组，研究利用商业程序和自然机器（如印刷和智能材料）来大幅度地降低成本，扩大电脑和传递的范围。

CC小组，研究数据世界的汽车发展。

智能柜台小组，专注于开发与数据相关的智能厨房。

格雷问题小组，考虑电脑与通讯对老龄人生活的影响。

宽频播放小组着重广播媒体的未来。

处理健康与电子商务的SIGS小组正在拓展中。

## 设施

媒体实验室是世界上仅有的几家电脑数量远远超过研究人员数目的实验室之一。一个用于实验的千兆比特光纤连接到带有各种各样电脑的网络，从微型的嵌入式处理器到超级电脑，包括由最主要的厂商开发的产品。能迅速提供样板的资源包括3-D印刷，喷射式制模和PC板制作。实验中心还设有语音与影视工作室，DNA排列实验室，新型传感器实验室，微波压缩和感性研究实验室。

## Massachussets Institute of Technology

### Retrospective

The outline of the Media Laboratory was formed in 1980 by Nicholas Negroponte and Jerome Wiesner, growing out of the Architecture Machine Group, and building on the seminal work of faculty members such as Marvin Minsky in cognition, Seymour Papert in learning, Barry Vercoe in music, Muriel Cooper in graphic design, Andrew Lippman in video, and Stephen Benton in holography. On October 1, 1985, it opened its doors for business in the newly designed I.M. Pei facility called the Wiesner Building.

In its first decade, much of the Laboratory's activity centered around abstracting electronic content from its traditional physical representations, helping create now-familiar areas such as digital video and multimedia.

The success of this agenda is now leading to a growing focus on how bits meet atoms: how electronic information overlaps with the everyday physical world. The Laboratory pioneered collaboration between academia and industry, and provides a unique environment to explore basic research and applications, without regard to traditional divisions among disciplines.

### Academic Programs

Unlike other laboratories at MIT, the Media Laboratory comprises both a degree granting academic program and a research program. The Laboratory's faculty and senior research staff number approximately 30; another 80 staff members also support the Laboratory's research, facilities, and administration. Graduate enrollment totals 164, divided nearly equally between master's and PhD candidates. Of these students, 138 are enrolled in the Media Arts and Sciences program, while another 26 are formally based in other MIT departments, but carry out their research under the direction of Media Laboratory faculty. In addition, approximately 150 undergraduates come to work at the Laboratory each year through MIT's Undergraduate Research Opportunities Program (UROP).

### Research Consortia

Much of the Laboratory's work today is organized into three main consortia, which are funded by corporate sponsors. Many of the technologies and applications conceived within the consortium structure are tested and refined through experiments at MIT and in the field, in cooperation with individual member companies.

Digital Life (DL) addresses the interconnection between bits, people, and things in an online world. Research focuses on four areas. Media/Performance defines structured representations of sound and pictures, merging networks with entertainment, and evolving our notions of storytelling. Actions/Interfaces explores speech, gestures, and motions, as well as immersive communications environments. Kids/Culture includes learning, construction, design, and cooperation by kids and adults of all ages and for all reasons. Connections/ Community builds environments for collaboration; discovery; design; and casual, global interactions.

The News in the Future (NiF) research consortium provides a forum for the MIT Media Laboratory and member companies to explore and exploit technologies that will improve the collection and dissemination of news. The goals are to enhance the efficiency of production, the timeliness of delivery, the convenience of presentation, and the relevance of editorial and advertising content to the consumer. NiF focuses on four areas: description of news by and for computers; observation and modeling of consumer behavior; presentation and interface design; and application. The consortium develops technologies for managing data, building linkages between news providers and consumers, and enabling new approaches to the look and feel of news content.

Things That Think (TTT), officially inaugurated at the Laboratory's 10th birthday celebration in October 1995, explores ways of moving computation beyond conventional sites, such as PCs or laptops, and adding intelligence to objects that are first and foremost something else. By sensing the movements or feelings of their owners - or by learning their owners' habits - common devices such as toasters, doorknobs, or shoes will be able, in their own right and through communication with one another, to solve meaningful problems. By becoming truly responsive and unobtrusive, the information technology in the inanimate things around us will enhance the quality of daily living. TTT brings together an unusual range of interdisciplinary talent and builds upon the close research partnership between the Laboratory and its sponsor community.

## Special Interest Groups

The Laboratory has also organized a growing number of smaller, more focused special interest groups (SIGs) which deal with particular subject areas. Six are currently in operation or formation: Toys of Tomorrow (TOT) explores ways that the digital revolution will transform the world of toys and play;

Penny PC investigates using commodity processes and natural mechanisms (e.g., printing and smart materials) to dramatically reduce the cost and expand the reach of computing and communications;

CC++ looks at cars in the digital world;

Counter Intelligence is focused on developing a digitally connected, self-aware kitchen;

Gray Matters considers the impact of computation and communication on the lives of older persons;

Broadercasting looks at the future of broadcast media.

SIGs dealing with health and e-commerce are in development.

## Facilities

The Media Laboratory is one of the few places in the world where computers outnumber people by a significant margin. An experimental, gigabit fiber-optic plant connects a heterogeneous network of computers, ranging from fine- grained, embedded processors to supercomputers, and includes products developed by most major manufacturers. The rapid prototyping resources include 3-D printing, injection molding, and PC board fabrication. There are studios for audio and video, and laboratories for DNA labeling, new sensors, micro-encapsulation and perceptual studies.

## 约翰・梅达

约翰・梅达，麻省理工学院媒体实验室设计与电脑专业副教授，索尼职业发展媒体艺术与科学教授。一九六六年生于西雅图，曾就读麻省理工学院，并获得电脑科学专业学士学位，一九八九年获硕士学位。约翰・梅达在日本筑波大学艺术设计学院完成了他的平面设计博士课程。在那里他开始试验把优秀平面设计的简洁与电脑设计的复杂性结合的概念，这些实验被编入一套名为《反应书》的五本系列书中，该书是当今世界公认的高质量数字媒体设计的标准。一九九六年，约翰为资生堂化妆品，索尼及森泽公司设计的商业作品在日本大坂DDD艺廊及东京GGG艺廊举办的"约翰・梅达：电脑与纸"个展中展出。最近，他编写了一本由麻省理工学院出版社出版的二百五十六页的《数字设计》，该书概述了他的作品作为平面案例与数码结合的理论基础。约翰・梅达与其合伙人基里斯・梅达共同经营位于麻省勒星顿的印刷及数码设计顾问公司－梅达工作室。

约翰・梅达所获的奖项包括：

"反应广场"获一九九四年日本多媒体荣誉大奖，为森泽设计的十幅系列海报获九六年东京字体指导俱乐部金奖，"十二点"获九七年东京字体俱乐部互动奖，为"ONE-LINE.COM"设计的项目获九九年日本文化部互动奖，一九九九年《ID》杂志金奖，一九九九年MILIA D'OR提名奖，"TAP，TYPE，WRITE"作品获一九九九年纽约艺术指导俱乐部新媒体金奖。约翰也是一九九九年DAIMLER-CHRYSLER设计奖的获得者。他的作品刊登在世界各地的刊物上，如《意念》、《AXIS》、《印刷》、《ARTBYTE》、《技术年鉴》、《ID》及《创作评论》。此外，他曾在各种机构进行演讲，如：索尼设计中心、三星IDS、东京设计中心、AXIS、东京字体指导俱乐部、GGG艺廊、DDD艺廊、INTERVAL研究机构、哈佛大学、普林斯顿大学、旧金山现代艺术博物馆、纽约艺术指导俱乐部及阿斯朋设计大会。

## John Maeda

John Maeda is Sony Career Development Professor of Media Arts and Sciences, Associate Professor of Design and Computation at the MIT Media Laboratory in Cambridge Massachusetts. He was born in Seattle, WA in 1966, and later attended MIT where he was awarded the bachelors and masters degrees in Computer Science in 1989. He completed his doctoral studies in graphic design at the Tsukuba University Institute of Art and Design in Tsukuba, Japan. There he began to experiment with ideas on ways to bond the simplicity of good graphic design together with the complex nature of the computer. Those experiments grew into a series of five books called "Reactive Books" that are today a worldwide-recognized standard for high quality digital media design. His commercial work for Shiseido Cosmetics, Sony, and Morisawa was honored in 1996 in the one-man exhibition "John Maeda: Paper and Computer" at the Ginza Graphic Gallery in Tokyo, Japan and the Dai Nippon Duo Dojima Gallery in Osaka, Japan. He recently published the 256-page book "Design By Numbers" from MIT Press which outlines the theoretical underpinnings of his work as a combination of graphical examples and codes. Together with his partner Kris Maeda, he runs the print and digital design consultancy MAEDASTUDIO in Lexington, MA. John Maeda's awards include the 1994 Japan Multimedia Grand Prix for "The Reactive Square," the 1996 Tokyo Type Director's Club Gold Prize for his series of 10 posters for Morisawa, the 1997 Tokyo Type Director's Club Interactive Prize for "12 o'clocks," the 1999 Japan Ministry of Culture Interactive Prize for "one-line.com," and the 1999 ID Magazine Gold Prize, the 1999 Milia d'Or nomination, and the 1999 New York Art Director's Club New Media Gold Award for "Tap, Type, Write." He is also a 1999 recipient of the Daimler-Chrysler Design Award. His work has been featured worldwide in periodicals such as IDEA, AXIS, Print, ArtByte, Technology Review, ID Magazine, and Creative Review. He has lectured at various venues including Sony Design Center, Samsung IDS, Tokyo Design Center, AXIS, Tokyo Type Director's Club, Ginza Graphic Gallery, Dai Nippon Duo Dojima Gallery, Interval Research, Harvard University, Princeton University, San Francisco Museum of Modern Art, The New York Art Directors Club, and the Aspen Design Conference.

# 麻省理工学院媒体实验室

约翰·梅达是麻省理工学院媒体实验室设计与电脑专业副教授，索尼职业发展媒体艺术与科学教授。他在实验室指导美学与电脑小组（ACG）。他的使命是促进他称之为“人文主义技术”的发展，即人们通过获知他们正运用的技术能够明确表达未来的文化。

ACG是一间实验研究工作室，于一九九六年成立，是前任教授穆里尔·库朋的可视语言室的再续。自它成立的短短时期里，ACG独特的实验作品以其在概念与工艺上的独创性，获得了众多奖项与赞誉。ACG成就的一个重要因素在于它以举行专题研讨会和活动的形式将基本的电脑技术概念介绍给艺术设计团体，如正进行的“数字设计”项目就是例证。

这里所介绍的设计师都参与了梅达工作室的教育项目。大多数的学生是研究生，有些是大学生，如本书封面作品的设计师马克斯·凡·克里克。梅达对过去与现在的小组成员深表感激，包括汤姆·怀特，阿瑟尔·基里安，戈兰·莱温，本杰明·佛莱，艾里斯·科，安得烈·得维特，梅根·格布莱夫，里察·斯特莱马特，周彼得及杰雷·舒夫曼。

including Tom White, Axel Kilian, Golan Levin, Ben Fry, Elise Co, Andre Devitt, Meagan Galbraith, Rich Streitmatter, Peter Cho and Jared Schiffman.

## 阿瑟尔·基里安

阿瑟尔·基里安是在ACG攻读建筑硕士学位的二年级学生，他正探索通过所指定图像空间获得数据空间的概念。一九九八年阿瑟尔获得德国柏林艺术大学建筑专业学位。

Axel Kilian is a second year Master's student in Architecture studies and the ACG group and is exploring the notion of digital space mediated through image space by using the point of attention. Axel received his professional degree in Architecture at the University of the Arts Berlin, Germany in 1998.

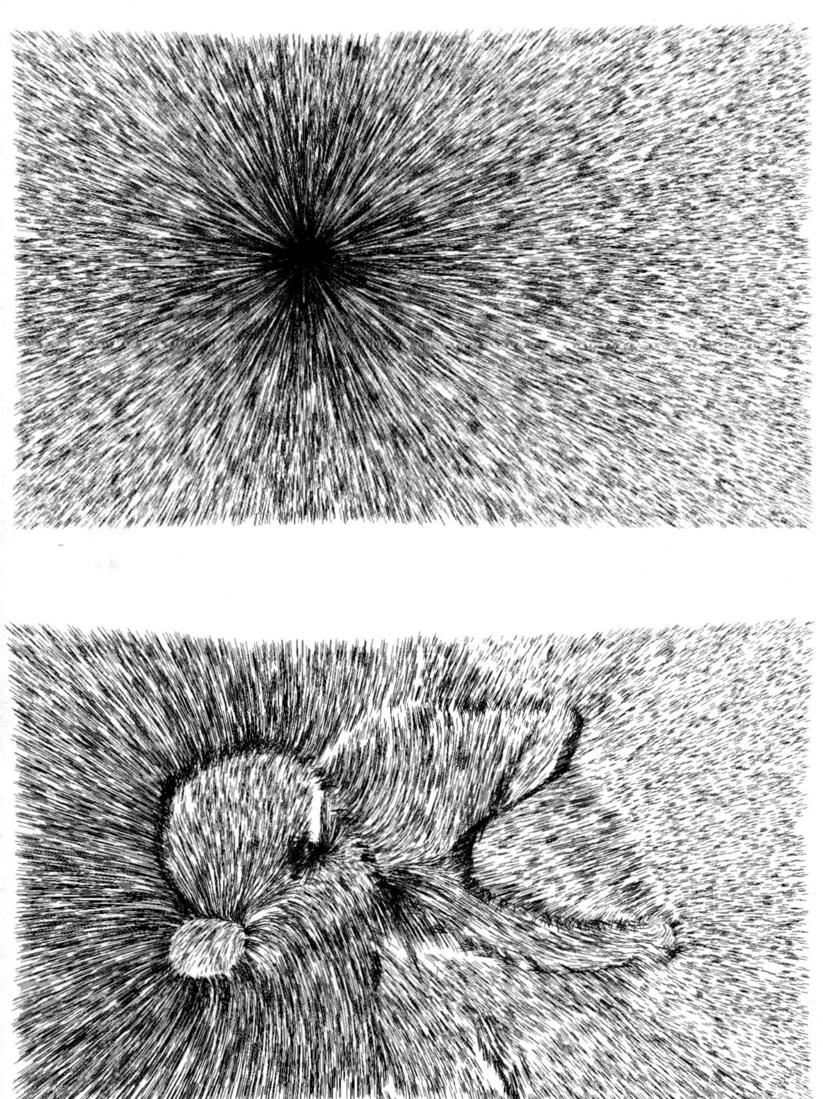

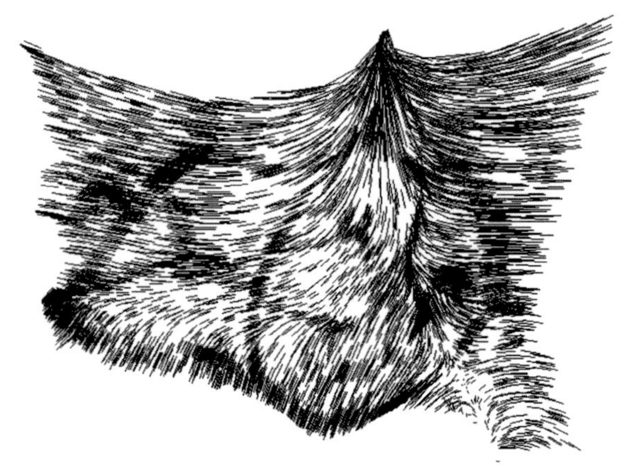

P15-17 指定点形成图像范围，视觉记忆通过时间变化而产生，根据线条的阴影及所指定点线距的不同线长而变化。留下来的痕迹是永久性的，并提醒图像范围内先前所做的移动。1999-2000

P15-17 The point of attention shapes the imagespace. Visual memory is created through the timevariation in the response of the cloud of lines and through their varying length based on the line's distance to the point of attention. The traces being left behind are permanent and remind of the previous moves in the image space.

## 周彼得

周彼得是旧金山的平面设计师及电脑程序员。最近在 IMAGINARY FORCES 公司工作，一间位于加州好莱坞的概念电影、广播与环境设计公司。

周在麻省理工学院获得媒体艺术与科学专业硕士及工程科学学士学位。作为麻省理工学院媒体实验室 ACG 的成员，在约翰教授的指导下，周专注于独立的研究项目来探索互动的可能性与暂存的字形。

他获得的奖项包括：一九九八年《ID》杂志互动媒体评论金奖，二零零零年东京字体指导俱乐部互动设计奖，入选《印刷杂志 2000 新视觉艺术家年鉴》。

Peter Cho is a graphic designer and computer programmer based in San Francisco. He has worked most recently at Imaginary Forces, a conceptual film, broadcast, and environmental design firm in Hollywood, California.

Cho holds a Master of Science degree in Media Arts and Sciences and a Bachelor of Science in engineering from the Massachusetts Institute of Technology. As a member of the Aesthetics and Computation Group at the MIT Media Laboratory, led by Professor John Maeda, Cho worked on independent research projects to explore the possibilities for interactive and temporal typographic forms.

His honors include a gold award in the 1998 ID Magazine Interactive Media Review, the 2000 Tokyo Type Directors Club Interactive Design Award, and inclusion in Print Magazine's 2000 New Visual Artists Review. His work can be seen online at www.pcho.net.

Jerome Wiesner, growing out of the Architecture Machine

electronic content from its traditional physical represent

how electronic information overlaps with the everyo

artificial and human intelligence: software

engineering of virtual communiti

funded by corporate sponsors

members also support th

What are the
A Sampling of Research
Work under way at the Media Laboratory represents
Advances in electronic paper, which may one day
New forms of data hiding (steganography), where digital
Wearable computing, where we move beyond
An entirely new approach to quantum computing
NetSoundTM, a new system built on the CSound
New ways of joining the physical environment
A new generation of toys to think with, including
Ways to interact with computers just as we interact
Field-sensing devices. One device, now
Perceptual audio models, which may revolutionize
An Audio Notebook, which uses sensors to
Intelligent scalability, which gives us new ways to create
Full-parallax holography, where you get the full
Intelligent agents that perform tasks ranging from
Intra-body signaling mechanisms that literally
Hyperinstrumentation, where the expressive range of
JIVE, a Joint Interactive Video Environment
Systems for device-to-device communication
Software editing systems that permit each viewer
Smart Rooms, which act like invisible butlers
More effective, meaningful online news services
Directed
A group of companies sponsor larger, directed research
AT&T Corp., BT, Hewlett-Packard, International Business
Several of these companies also support fellowships
The Media Laboratory is one of the few places in the world
Financial
The Media Laboratory's annual budget is approximately
February
s for audio and video, and laboratories for electromagnetics, materials, optics,
aboratory and into worldwide use. Geographically, 50 percent of the Laboratory's sponsors
MIT Media Laboratory
enabling technologies for understanding and expression by people
The Media Laboratory was formed in 1980 by Nicholas
In its first decade, much of the Laboratory's activity centered
The success of this agenda is now leading to a growing focus on
Unlike other laboratories at MIT, the Media Laboratory
Learning and Common Sense includes theoretical and
Perceptual Computing embraces human and machine
Information and Entertainment ranges from the basic
Academic
The Laboratory's faculty and senior research staff number
Research
The Laboratory's work today is organized into
addresses the interconnection between bits
culty. In addition

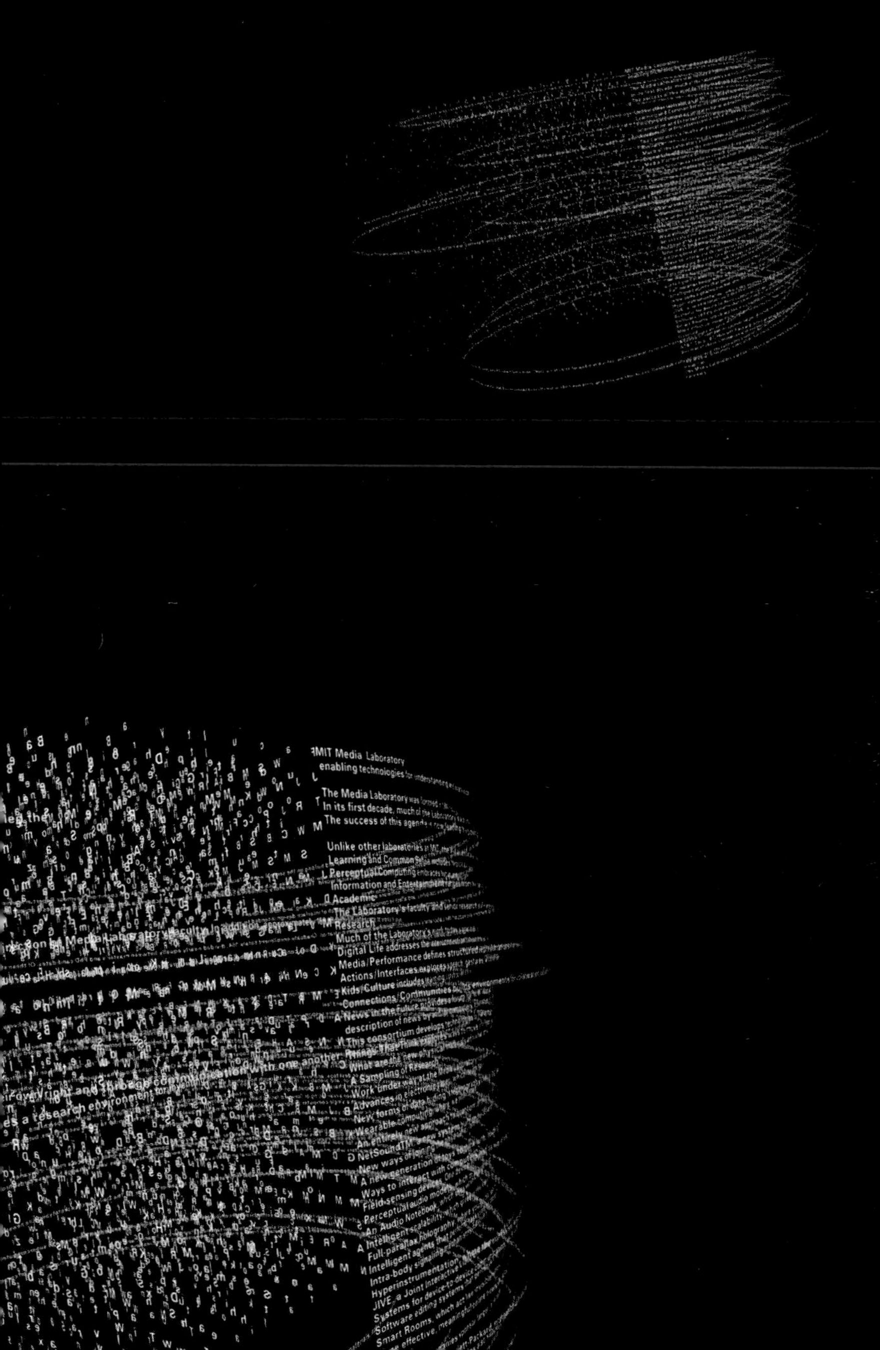
MIT Media Laboratory
enabling technologies
The Media Laboratory
In its first decade, much of the Laboratory
The success of this agenda
Unlike other laboratories
Learning and Common Sense
Perceptual Computing
Information and Entertainment
Academic
The Laboratory's faculty and senior research
Research
Much of the Laboratory's
Digital Life addresses the
Media/Performance defines structured
Actions/Interfaces explores
Kids/Culture includes
Connections/Communities
News in the Future provides
description of news
This consortium develops
Things That Think
What are the new physical
A Sampling of Research
Work under way at the
Advances in electronic
New forms of data
Wearable computing
An entirely new approach
NetSound
New ways of
A new generation
Ways to interact with
Field-sensing devices
Perceptual audio models
An Audio Notebook
Intelligent scalability
Full-parallax holography
Intelligent agents that
Intra-body signaling
Hyperinstrumentation
JIVE, a Joint Interactive
Systems for device-to-device
Software editing systems
Smart Rooms, which act
effective, meaningful

now-familiar areas such as digital video and
ilding on the seminal work of faculty members such as Marvin Minsky in cognition, Seymour Papert
ld. The Laboratory pioneered collaboration between academia and industry
erstanding, and how children
of interface design intended to include
sign, object-oriented and holographic video; and tools for creative
ation. Graduate enrollment totals 164, divided nearly equally between master's
cations conceived within the consortium structure are tested and refined
dissemination of news. The goals include enhancing the efficiency of production
d feel
re responsive to people's everyday wants and needs. By sensing
n-design and storytelling. In the past, new technologies were born in the workplace, and ended up in toys. In the future
l systems? How can such systems be used to solve longstanding personal and social
ink" made of tiny particles that are black on one side and white on the other
identification, annotation, or copyright
et, complete with MIDI synthesizer and pocket speakers. Other clothes could have
s so effectively that it would turn today's largest supercomputer into a digital
ckly on the Internet, allowing the delivery of music at many hundreds, even thousands
ps, and eventually through household surfaces like refrigerator
nd probability, that were seen as too complex for kids in the pre-digital
aracters capable of face-to-face interaction
ear-facing or forward-facing baby seat, signaling an airbag when and when not to
ngle computer program capable of generating high-quality sound effects
notes, and the greater flexibility in design
. This work allows greater
or the side
take on new digital meanings
are currently reading or writing on

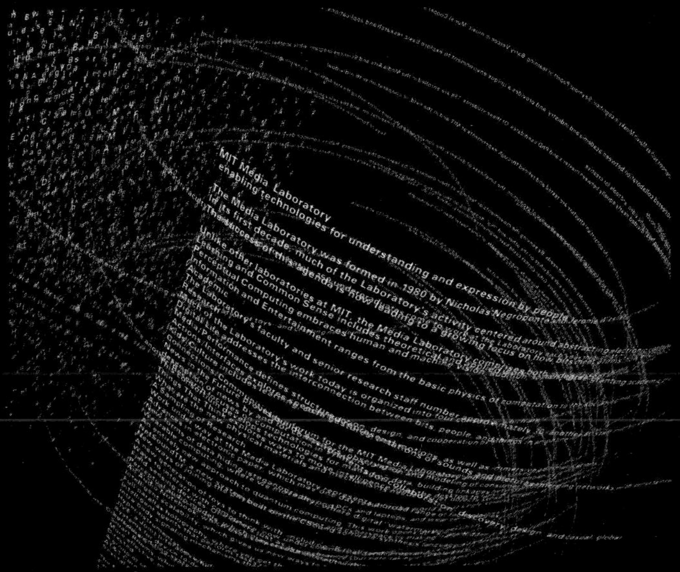

MIT Media Laboratory
enabling technologies for understanding and
The Media Laboratory was formed in 1980 by Nicholas
In its first decade, much of the Laboratory's activity
The success of this agenda is now leading to a growing
Unlike other laboratories at MIT, the Media Laboratory
Learning and Common Sense includes theoretical and applied
Perceptual Computing embraces human and machine vision
Information and Entertainment ranges from the basic physics of
Academic
The Laboratory's faculty and senior research staff number
Research
Much of the Laboratory's work today is organized into
Digital Life addresses the interconnection between bits, people
Media/Performance defines structured representations of sound
Actions/Interfaces explores speech, gestures
Kids/Culture includes learning
Connections/Communities builds environments for collaboration, discovery
News in the Future provides a forum
description of news by and for computers
This consortium develops technologies
Things That Think explores ways to move intelligence
What are the new physical materials and mechanisms
A Sampling of Research
Work underway at the Media Laboratory represents
Advances in electronic paper, which may one day
New forms of data hiding (steganography
Wearable computing, where we move beyond
An entirely new approach to quantum computing
NetSoundTM, a new system built on the CSound
New ways of joining the physical environment
A new generation of toys to think with, including
Ways to interact with computers, just as we
Field-sensing devices. One device
Perceptual audio models, which may revolutionize
An Audio Notebook, which uses sensors
Intelligent scalability, which gives us new ways to
Full-parallax holography, where you get the full
Intelligent agents that perform tasks ranging from
Intra-body signaling mechanisms that literally

Back to the Future?
Tell me.
Don't get me wrong
Does this make
The Case of City of Bits
In 1995 I had a chance to explore these
We made the marketing people happy by
We provided free access to the Web version.
Why should this be so?
The answer is that the hardback and
Hardback
Paperback
No-back
Of course
With the
You may also want a well designed
As forward-looking computer technologists
Getting the Reader's Attention
The first task of a book especially a trade book
The Web version clearly had to attract attention
The Web version clearly had to attract attention in the MIT Press
Hot-links from other Web sites provide a second
The third strategy for bringing in readers is to attract the
A fourth possible strategy
Reading Tools and their Effects
In traditional fashion
The physical book is not only a repository of the textual
The online version provides very different
The hierarchy of information is
Endnotes
Overall
Fixed-Format and Personalized
Good graphic designers exert very considered
But the client-server architecture of the Web
The issue of producer-control versus user
External Hot-Links
Perhaps the most obvious and striking difference
Some of these external hot-links
The converse process
Superficially
But the most important difference
As the Web and similar structures
Marginalia and Readers' Comments
City of Bits

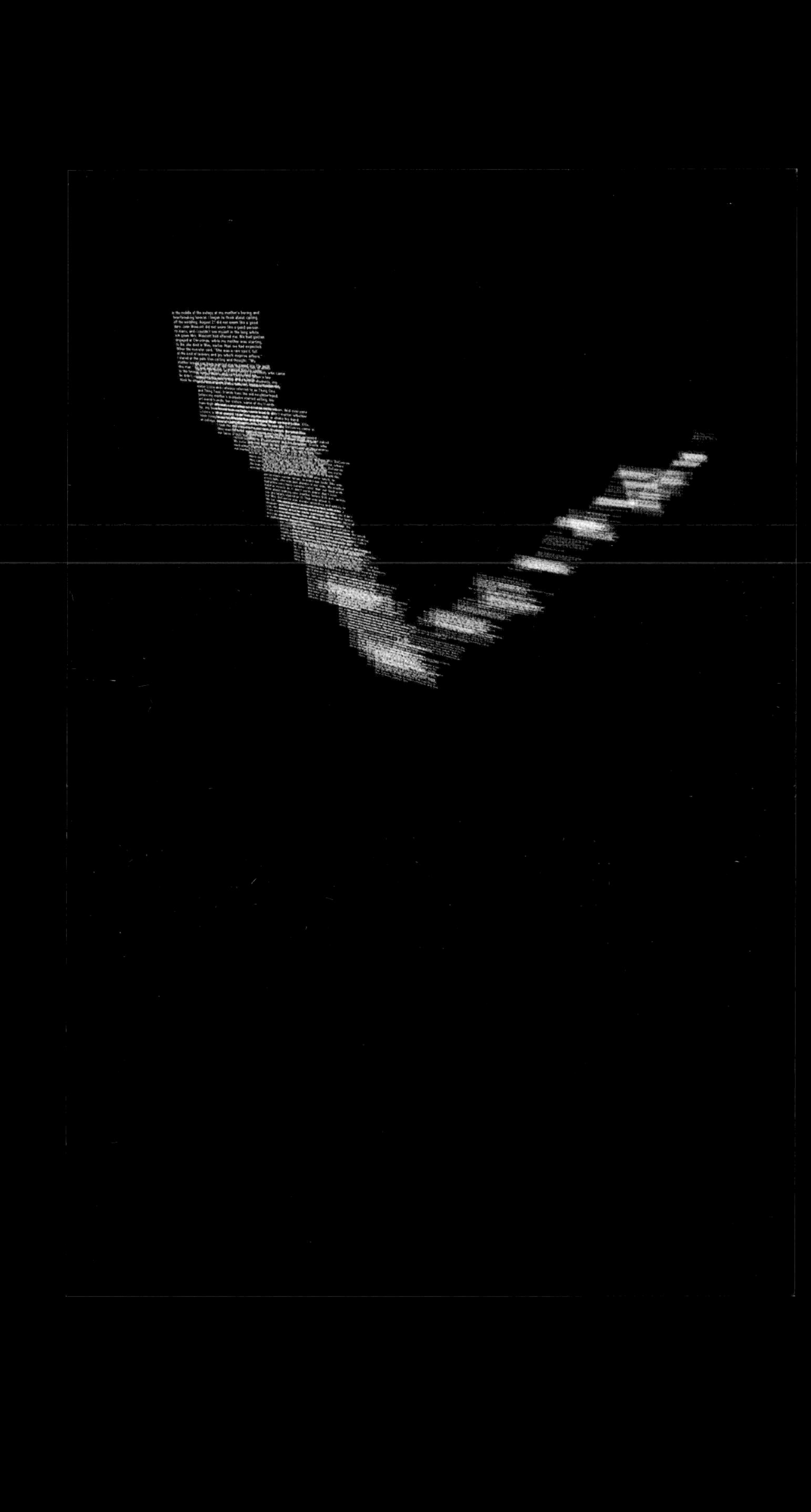

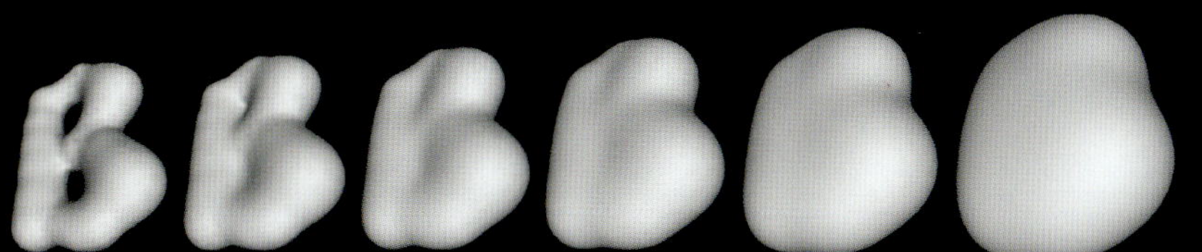

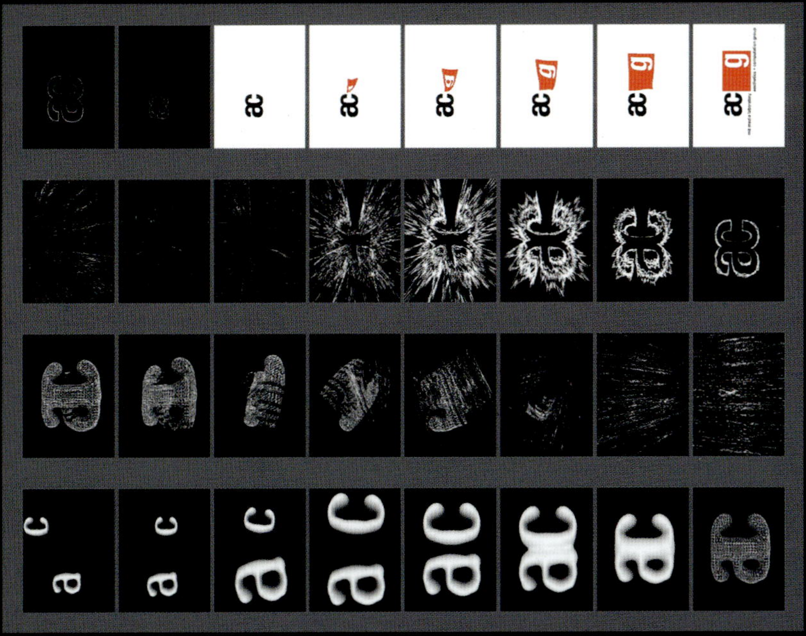

The Crooked God

the other gods

the other gods played tricks

at his feet when he walked

He seemed so absurd, this shepherd' crook,

his head

To see to either side

The crooked god

only to see the other gods laughing

One day, as he walked along the horizon,

he stepped over a snail

that was crossing his path.

*Let me repay you for not treading on me*

How can you possibly repay me?

Put me inside your ear and you shall see.

No sooner was the snail inside the god's ear

Watch out for the tree ahead.

*Pay no attention,* said the snail

as the crooked god walked toward a thicket

*The way is clear.*

Step to the left, whispered the snail

or you will

yourself on a thornbush.

And that is how two can change what one cannot

From that day on the crooked god walked as if he wer

ABCDE
FGHIJK
LMNOP
QRSTU
VWXYZ

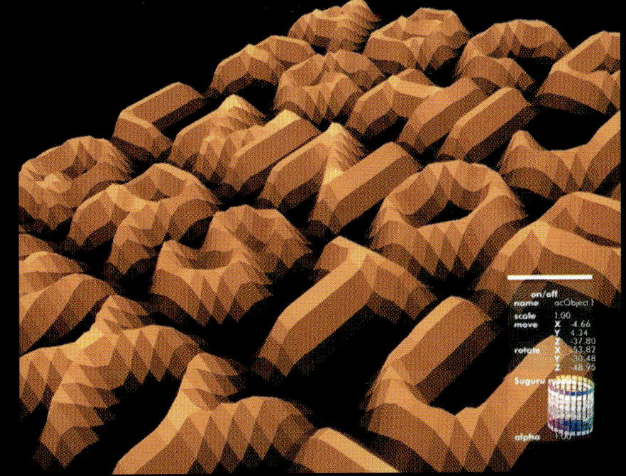
on/off
name acObject1
scale 1.00
move X 4.66
Y 4.34
Z 37.80
rotate X
Y
Z
Suguru
alpha

CHO: STOP THINKING SO FLAT.

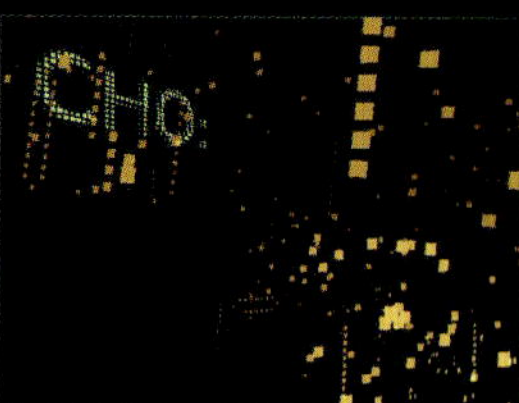

P19-35 "TYPERACTIVE"

字体与字体设计的实验。"摆弄"一个字母是什么意思呢？当文字出现在虚拟的空间或当字形对输入作出反应会发生什么呢？单一的标记如何在多维参数中——运动、相互作用、空间、时间——同时存在？形状又如何影响信息？这些设计经验回答了部分的问题，但又提出了更多的问题。

一九九六年至一九九九年，在约翰·梅达教授的指导下，彼得·周在麻省理工学院媒体实验室ACG拓展了这些图象所代表的设计研究。

P19-35 "Typeractive"

Experiments in typography and type design. What does it mean to "play" a letter? What happens when text appears in a virtual space? Or when letterforms can react and adapt to gestural input? How can a single mark exist in many dimensions - motion, interaction, space, time - at the same time? How does the form affect the message? These design experiments answer some of these questions but ask many more.

These images represent design research developed by Peter Cho from 1996 to 1999 at the MIT Media Lab's Aesthetics and Computation group, under the direction of Prof. John Maeda.

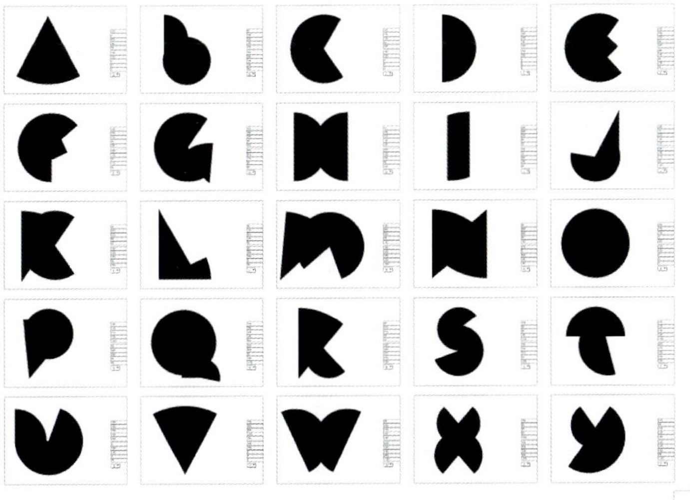

A B C D E
F G H I J
K L M N O
P Q R S T
U V W X Y Z

ALPHABET

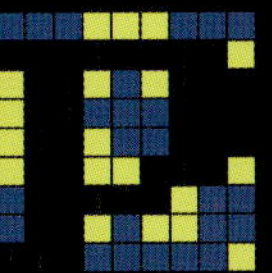

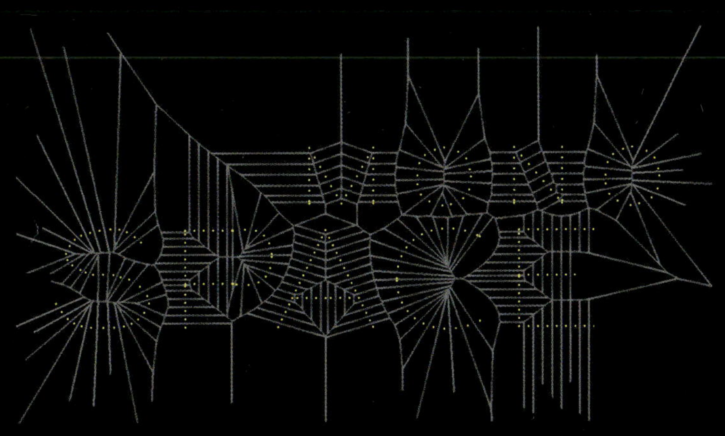

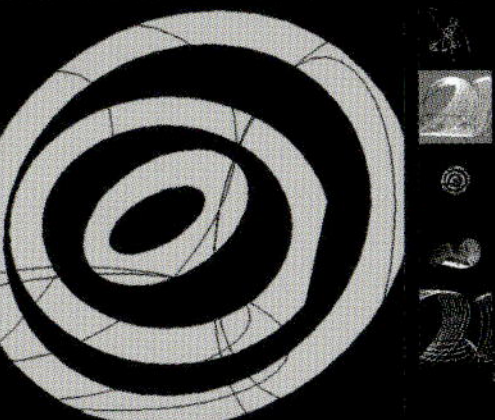

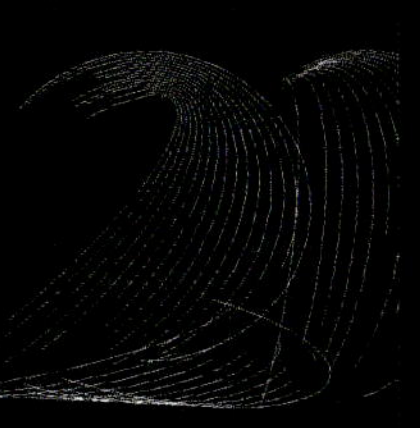

## 戈兰・莱温

戈兰・莱温是一位艺术家与设计师，对创作手工艺品，探索视听与非语言表达的流畅新模式环境颇感兴趣。戈兰获得麻省理工学院媒体实验室 ACG 硕士学位。在此之前，他作为一名研究科学家与互动设计师在 INTERVAL 研究机构工作了四年。戈兰曾在众多的地点举办互动艺术作品展览，包括 SIGGRAPH 1996 及 2000 艺术展，ISEA 1997，1997 与 2000 ARS ELECTRONICA，圣・荷塞创新技术博物馆，美国动画博物馆。他是国际 2000 PRIX ARS ELECTRONICA 的优异奖获得者。戈兰现与亚力山大・格尔曼一起在纽约市的〝设计机器〞公司工作。

Golan Levin is an artist and designer interested in creating artifacts and environments that explore supple new modes of audiovisual and nonverbal expression. Golan received his Master's degree from the Aesthetics and Computation Group at the MIT Media Laboratory; prior to this, he worked as a research scientist and interaction designer at Interval Research Corporation for four years. Golan has exhibited interactive artworks at numerous venues, including the SIGGRAPH 1996 and 2000 Art Shows, ISEA 1997, Ars Electronica 1997 and 2000, the San Jose Tech Museum of Innovation, and the American Museum of the Moving Image. He is the recipient of the Award of Distinction in the international 2000 Prix Ars Electronica. Golan now works with Alexander Gelman at Design Machine in New York City.

戈兰・莱温目前的工作已集中于互动设计，这些设计可让人们在一定时间内创造抽象的动画和声音。莱温的视听环境室展现他对一种表现方式的观点，这种表现方式是将绘画程序与乐器结合。实验室的每一个作品都是设计一种界面的实验尝试，既灵活又容易掌握，同时可在形象与声音中产生无穷无尽变化与个性表达的视听效果。

Golan Levin's recent work has focused on the design of interactions which allow people to create abstract animation and sound in real time. Levin's Audiovisual Environment Suite represents his vision of a performance medium that merges paint programs with musical instruments. Each artwork in the suite is an experimental attempt to design an interface which is both supple and easy to learn, yet also yields inexhaustibly variable and personally expressive audiovisual performances in both image and sound.

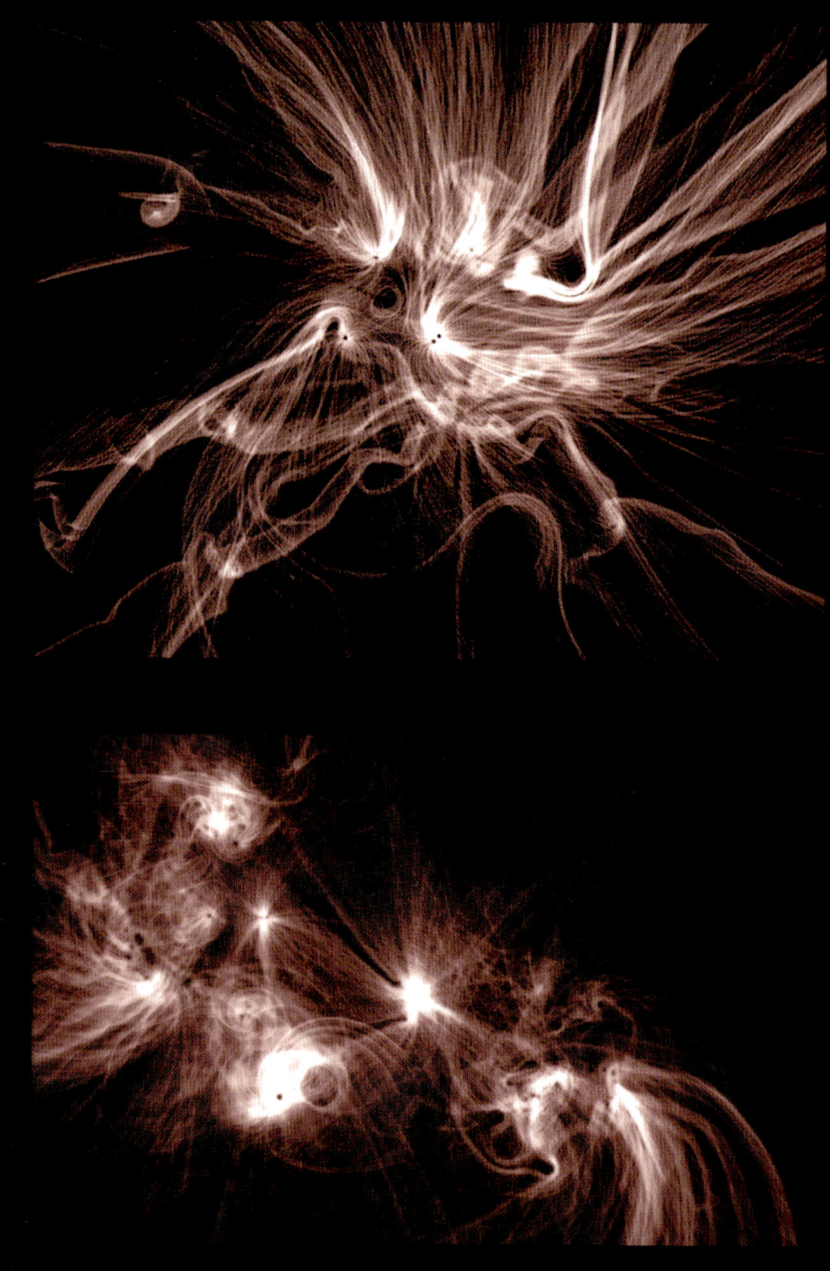

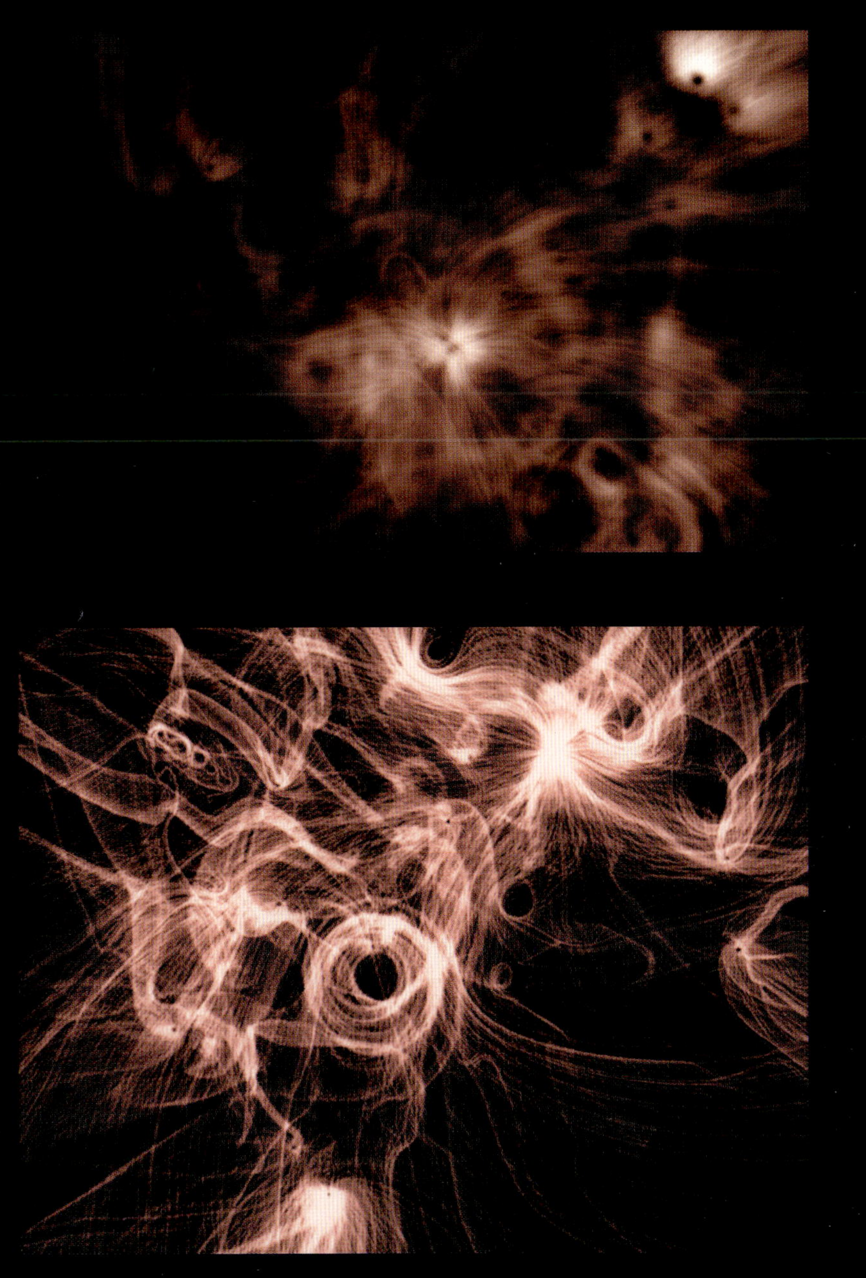

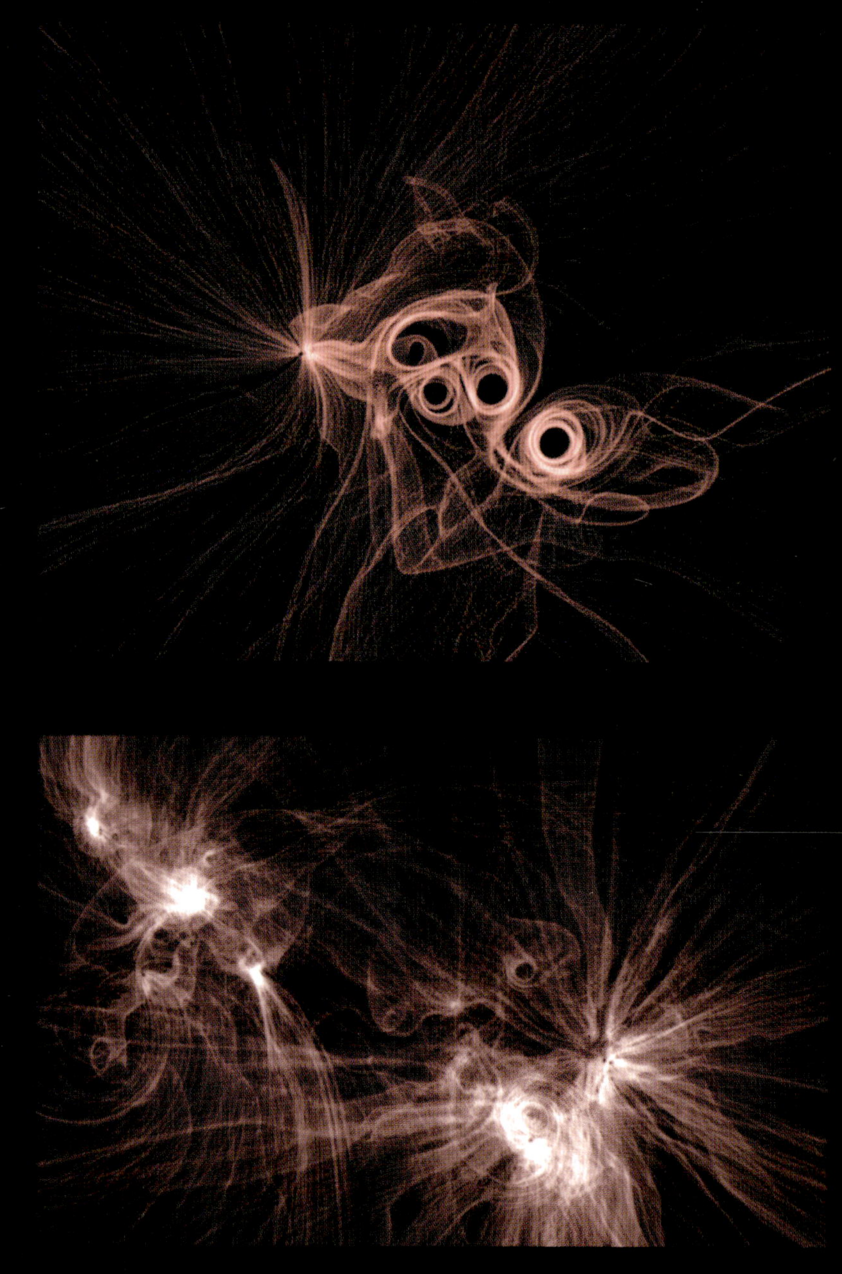

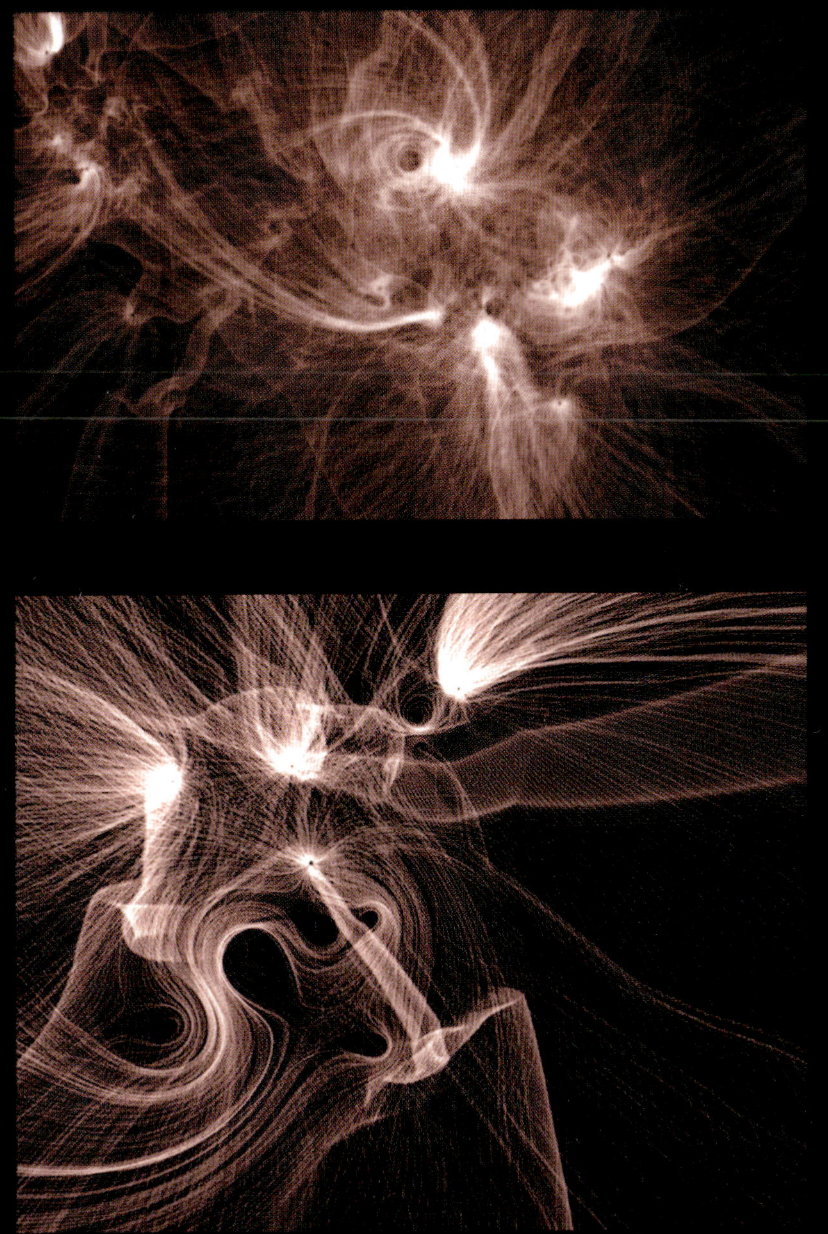

## P37-41 "FLOO"

一种互动视听环境，围绕 NAVIER-STOKES 流体流动模式而建立，用者通过储存一系列的流动奇点，然后引领大量微粒穿越由这些奇点建立的流动场，创造模拟合成声音与图像。由这些微粒留下的冷光痕迹逐渐形成一个图像，同时声音由颗粒合成器形成，其参数由这些微粒的属性决定。

P37-41 "Floo"

It is an interactive audiovisual environment constructed around a Navier-Stokes simulation of fluid flow. Users create synthetic sound and image by depositing a series of fluid singularities (sources and vortices) across the terrain of the screen, and then steering a large quantity of particles through the flow field established by these singularities. An image is gradually built up from the luminescent trails left by the particles; at the same time, sound is generated by a granular synthesizer whose parameters are governed by the dynamic properties of these particles.

## P42 "DIRECTRIX"

1998年的夏季与初秋，戈兰重新研究线条并拓展了 DIRECTRIX。DIRECTRIX 可让用者快速绘制生动的仿真抛物线，这些复杂的曲线是用者以动、静动作形成的。当几种曲线叠在一起，结果各不相同，有些是零散柔和的精致曲线，有些则是剧烈抖动的浓密的线团。

P42 "Directrix"

In the summer and early fall of 1998, Golan returned to the study of lines and developed Directrix, an environment in which users can quickly generate animated pseudo-parabolas. These complex curves are the result of an interplay between a set of dynamic and static gestures performed by the user. When several of these curves are layered together, the results can vary from sparse and delicate constructions of gently curved lines, to violently twitching, thatchy masses.

P45-47 "FLOCCUS"

1999年1月，戈兰开始研究动态的平面线有可能传递仿真的物质感觉的方式。经过一些实验，戈兰发明了一种模型来表现实物线条的基本结构，其中的一个限定元素，聚集弹簧阻尼器（制音器）模式是由连接在可变线条的一些小颗粒及弹簧组成，他发明的这个模型有模仿可伸缩细丝的效果，比如头发或细丝。在FLOCCUS（拉丁语"毛团"）里，用者所画的细丝围绕鼠标移动形成的想像轴转动。

P45-47 "Floccus"

In January of 1999 Golan began to study the means by which dynamic graphical lines might become able to convey a plausible sense of physicality. After some experimentation he developed a model for representing the underlying structure of physical lines, in which a finite-element, mass-spring-damper simulation is composed of virtual particles connected by alternating linear and torsional springs. The model he developed has the effect of simulating the tensile properties of thin physical filaments, such as hairs or twigs. In Floccus (the name is a Latin term for hairball), ductile filaments drawn by the user swirl around a shifting, imaginary drain centered at the user's cursor.

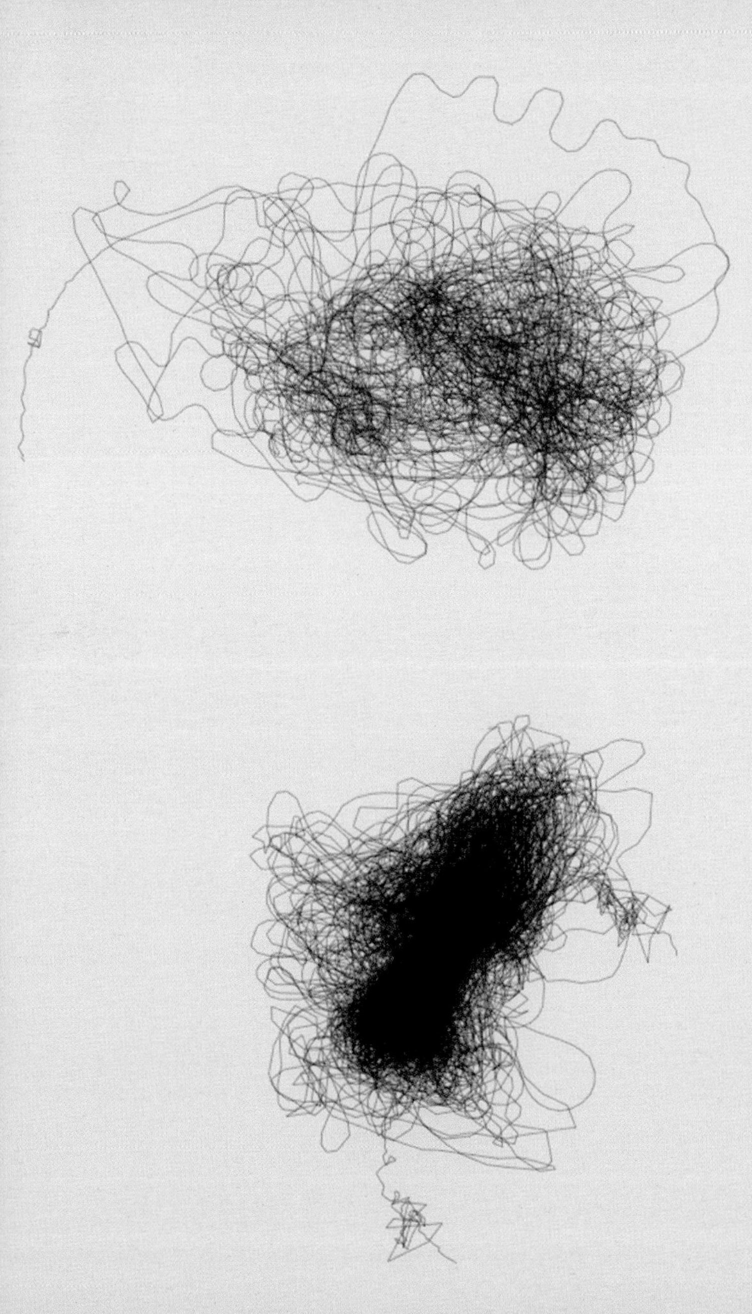

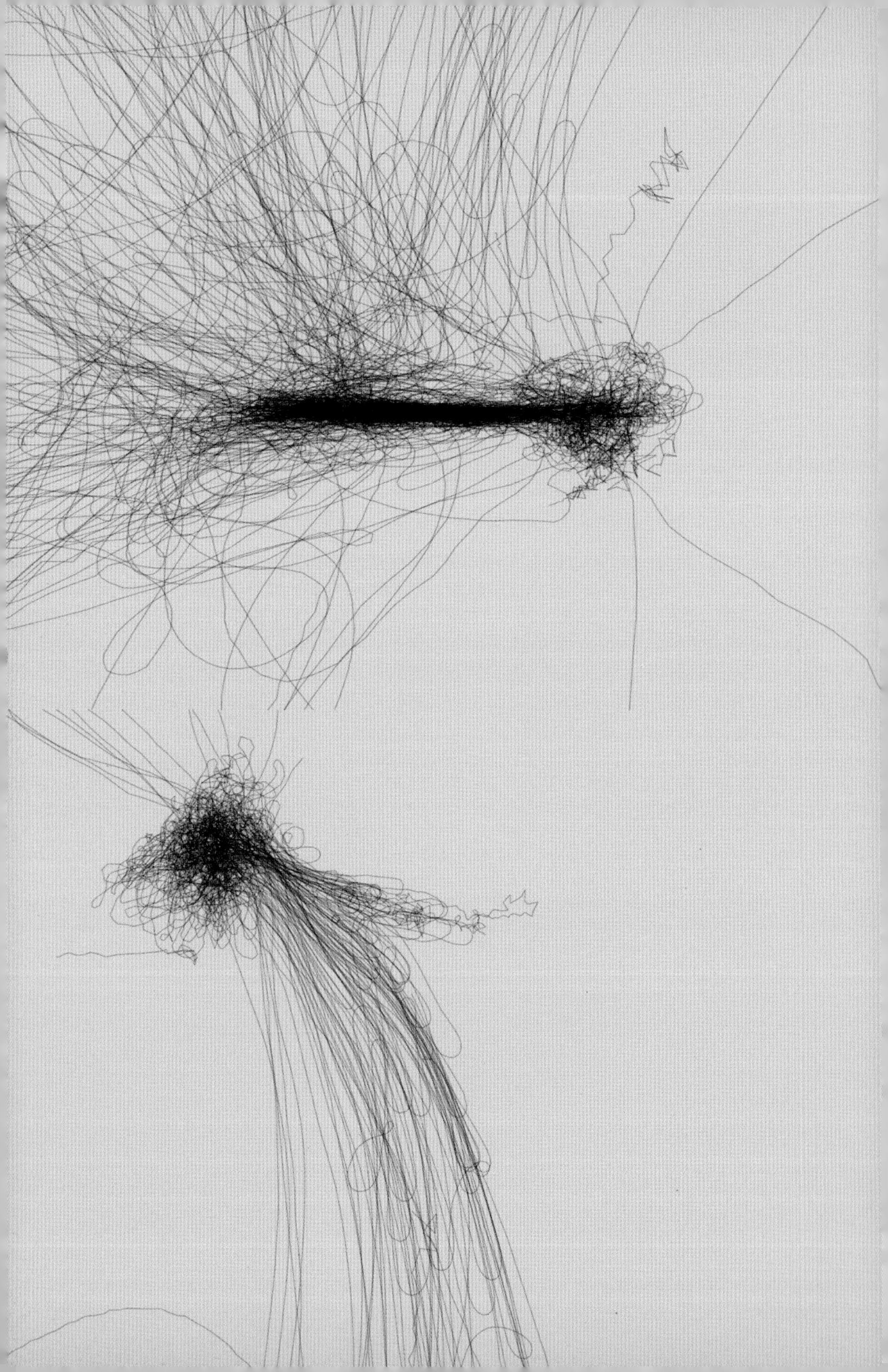

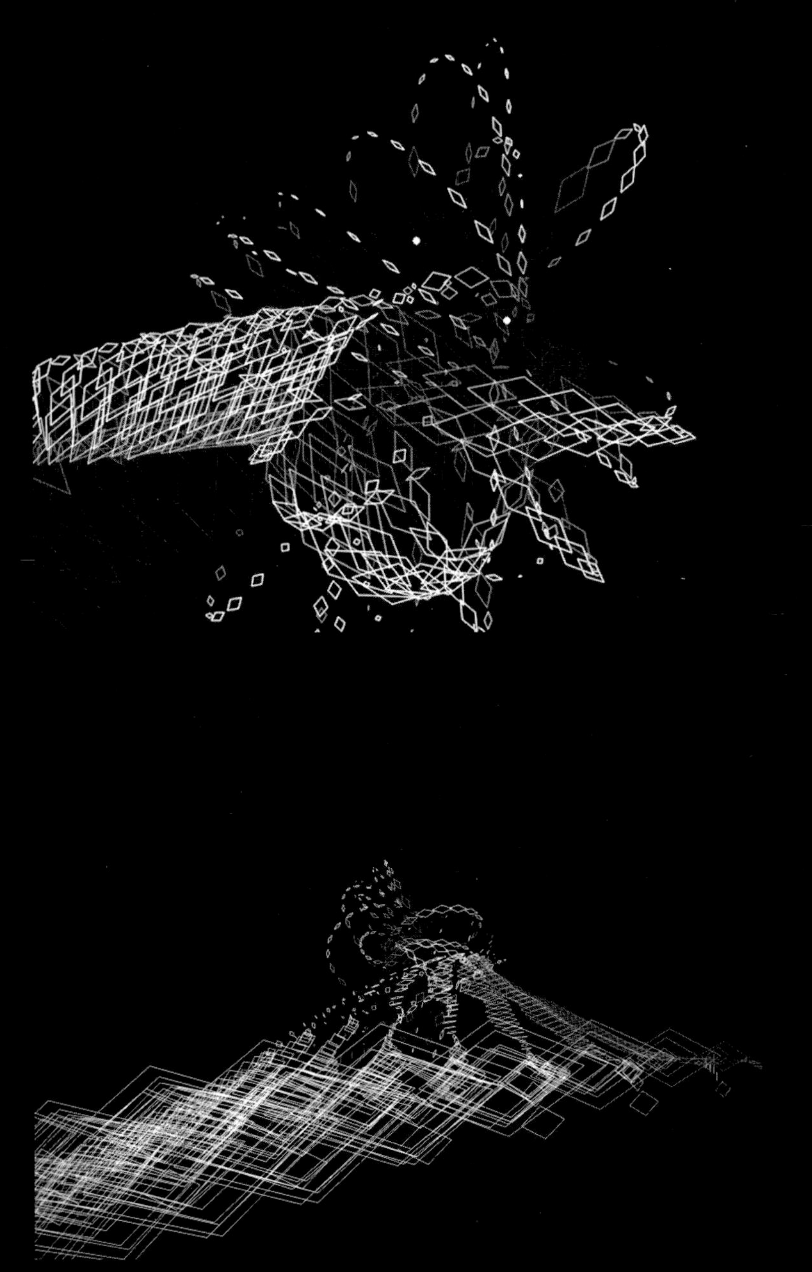

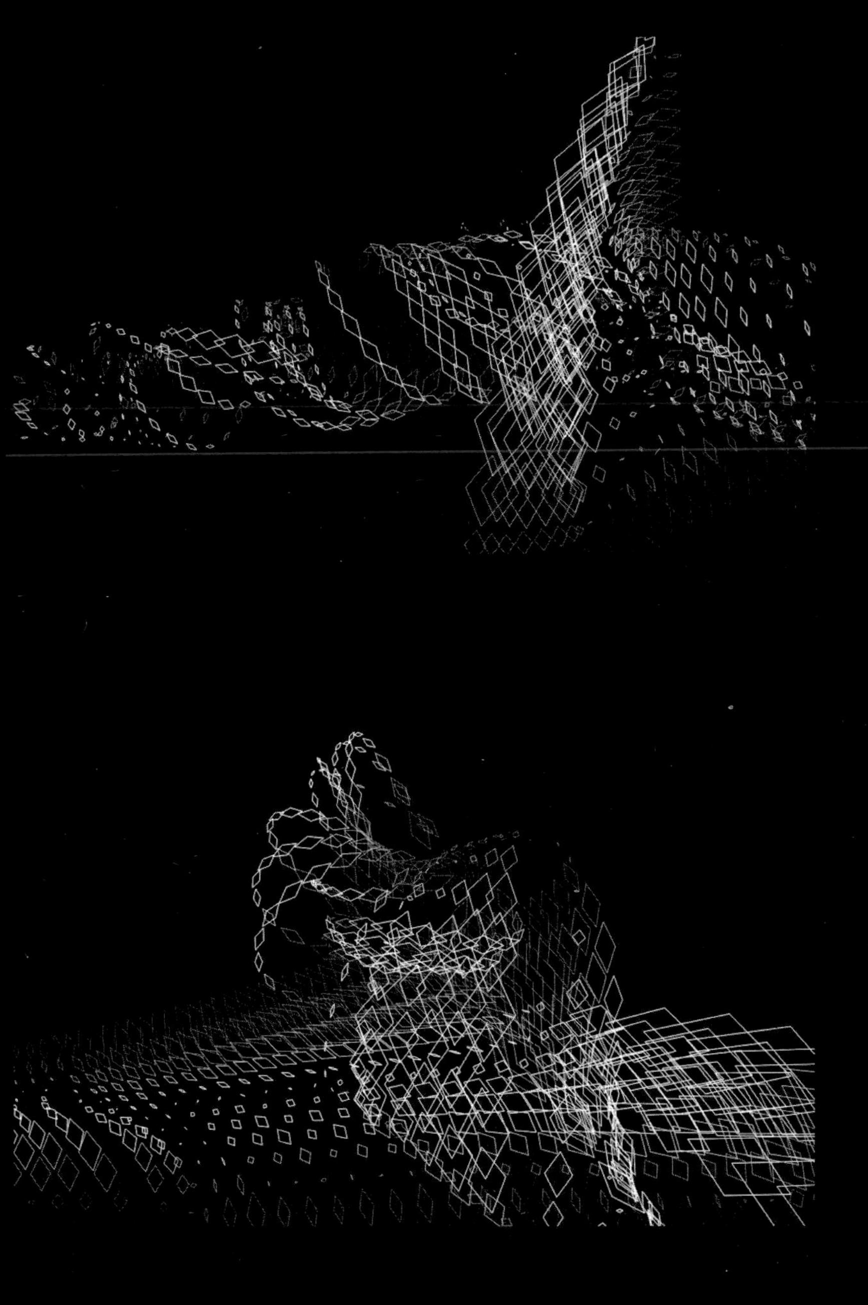

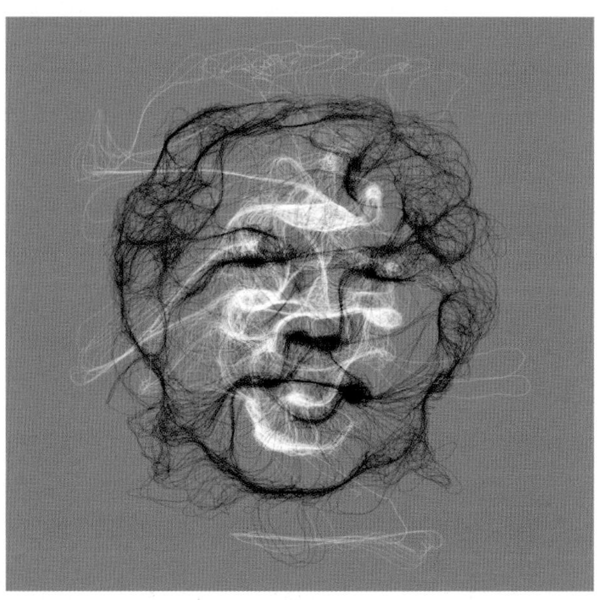

P48-49 "网"，1998

网是一种互动绘图软件，用者的笔画构成薄沙似的动画元素网，并可随意改变这种网状结构。

P48-49 "Meshy", 1998

It is an interactive drawing environment in which the user's strokes scaffold a gauzy mesh of animated elements. Users can gesturally tease and torque the mesh in real-time.

P50 "BRILLO系统制作的FLOCCULAR肖像"

在BRILLO系统中，用者绘画的线条受到来自照片一种隐藏力的打击。浅色细线被吸引到照片的明亮部位，而黑色细线则被吸引到照片的阴暗部位。戈兰采用这些简单的规则，把一堆随意的涂鸦与几张同事的肖像合并。其结果是细微的、有机的、有时是不规则的转变：头发的阴暗形成对比。其后他了解到类似的技巧，把线条组合表现图像中的侧面斜度，这个技巧被拓展为电脑视觉领域中的一种边缘监测规则。这种方式称为"活跃轮廓线"或"蛇"。

P50 "Floccular Portraits made in the Brillo System"

In Brillo, lines drawn by the user are buffeted by forces derived from a hidden but underlying photograph. Light-colored filaments are attracted to bright regions of the photograph, while dark filaments are attracted to dark regions. Golan used these simple rules to coalesce piles of casual scribbles into several portraits of his colleagues. The results are wispy, organic and sometimes unsettling transformations: chiaroscuros in hair. Later, he learned that a similar technique, of compelling lines to perform lateral gradient descents on an image, had been developed as an edge-detection algorithm in the field of computer vision, where the method is called "active contours" or "snakes."

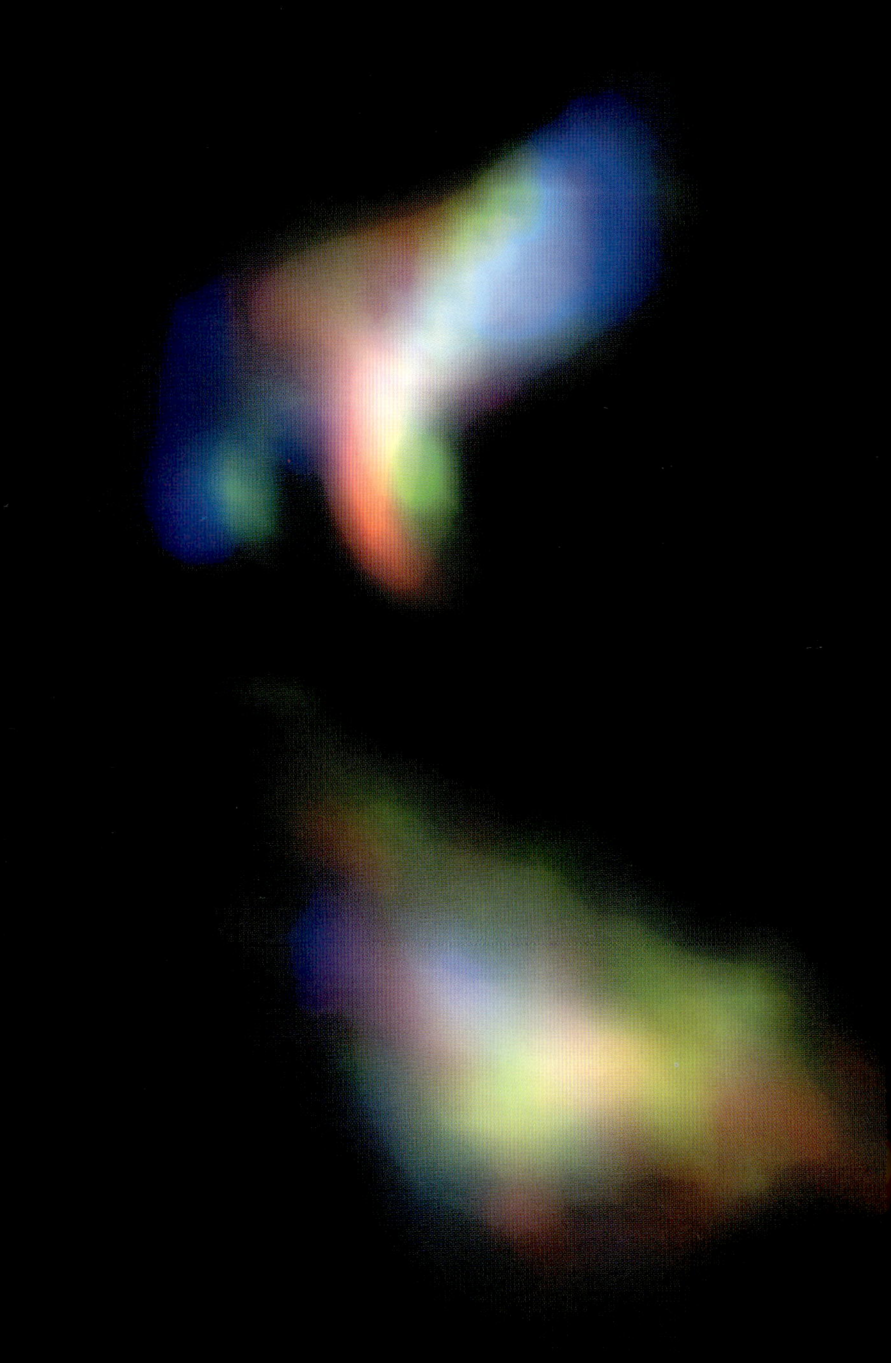

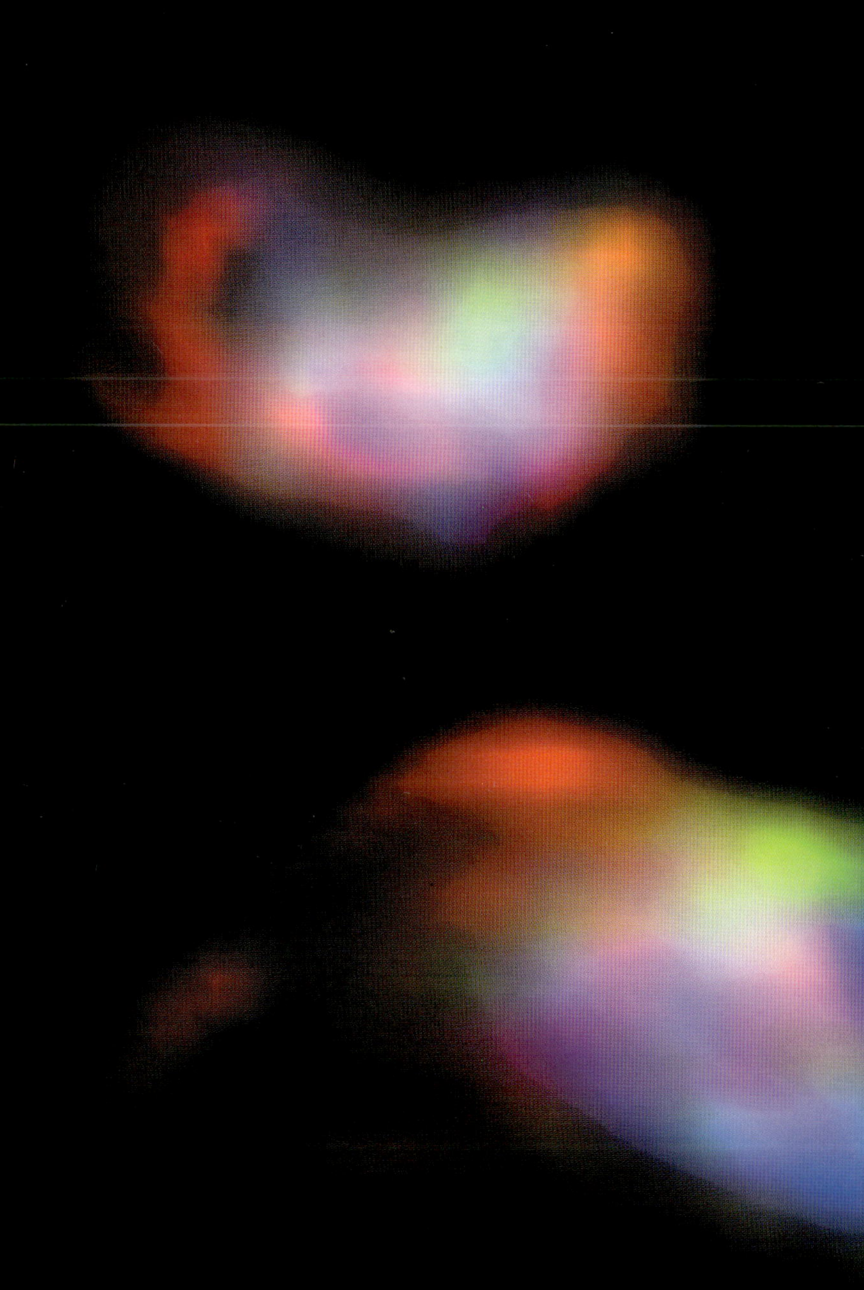

P52-53 "奥罗拉"

1999年1月的一天，戈兰没戴眼镜正在用毛团（FLOCCUS）画图时，突然发现毛团的构成微粒形成的密集画面本身就是一副有趣的展示。于是"奥罗拉"由此诞生，它是一种互动系统，底层色的构成是毛团的模拟，但其视觉展示包括了"模糊"、"发微光"、"云雾状"的效果，"奥罗拉"产生的无形形状随着用者的动作快速形成、消失及消散。

P52-53 "Aurora"

One day in February 1999, while playing with the Floccus without his eyeglasses on, it occurred to Golan that the density map of Floccus's constituent particles might itself make an interesting display. Thus was born Aurora, a reactive system whose structural underpainting is a floccular simulation, but whose visual display consists instead of a blurry, shimmering, nebulous cloud. Aurora's glowing formlessness rapidly evolves, dissolves and disperses as it follows and responds to the users movements.

P54 "WARBO"

WARBO是一种快速实验，戈兰把一些旧的设计片断结合成一个新整体。在WARBO系统中，用者创造一组彩色生动的斑点，每个点对应于一个正弦波音。一个双手操作的界面将鼠标的作用和WACOM显示板结合在一起，然后让用者控制怎样使这些音调可听得见。

P54 "Warbo"

Warbo was a quick experiment in which Golan combined a number of old design fragments into a new whole. In Warbo, the user creates a group of colored animated spots, each of which corresponds to a pure sine tone. A two-handed interface, which combines the use of a mouse and a Wacom tablet, then allows users to control how these tones are made audible.

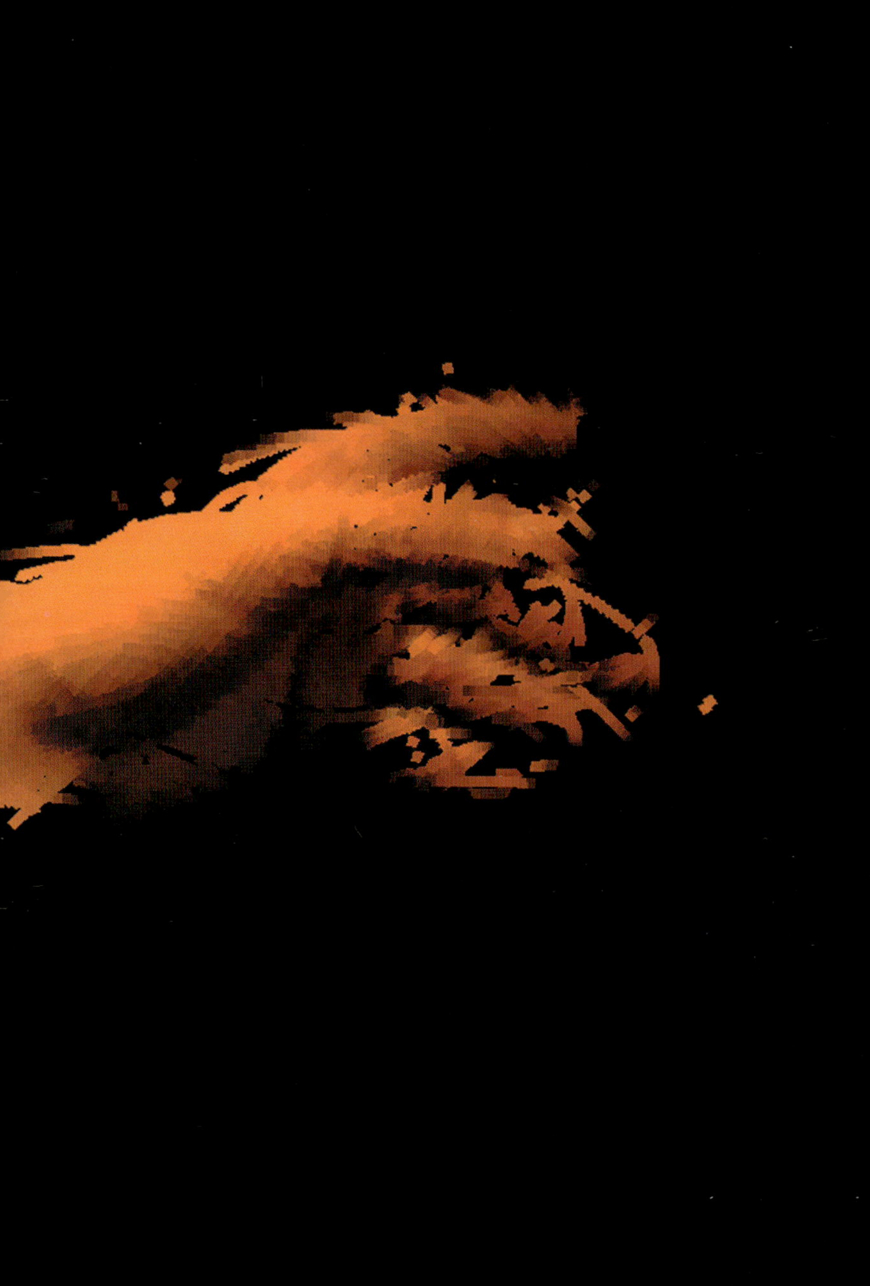

P56/P58-59 “摄影”

1998年秋，梅达教授就“数字摄影”开设了课程，重点是在捕捉感觉、摆弄画面与互动情形下的电脑表达。配上低精度的数码相机，学生每周编写软件项目来探索在信号处理及互动设计上的美学问题。在一学期的课程里，学生们创造了一百多个 JAVA APPLETS 软件，其中很多是互动的，为在电脑中处理图像提供新途径。戈兰的几张定格画面展示在这里。

P56/P58-59 "Numeric Photography Applets"

In the fall of 1998, Professor Maeda taught a class in "Numeric Photography," which focused on computational expression in the context of scenecapture, image-play, and interaction. Equipped with low-end digital cameras, students created weekly software projects to explore aesthetic issues in signal processing and interaction design. Over the course of the semester, the students created more than a hundred Java applets - many of which are interactive - that suggest new avenues for image - play on the computer. Several stills from a few of Golan's own applets are shown here.

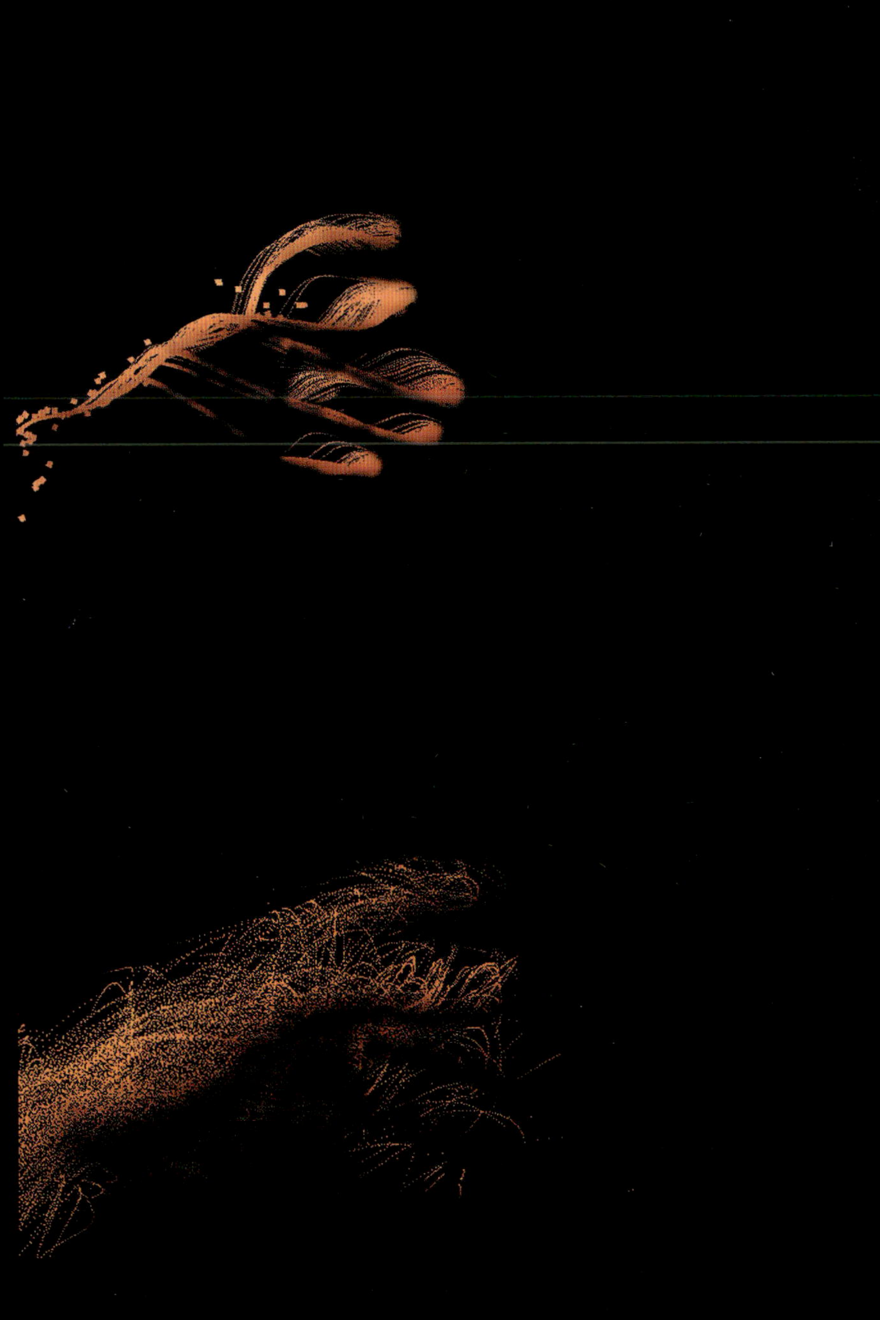

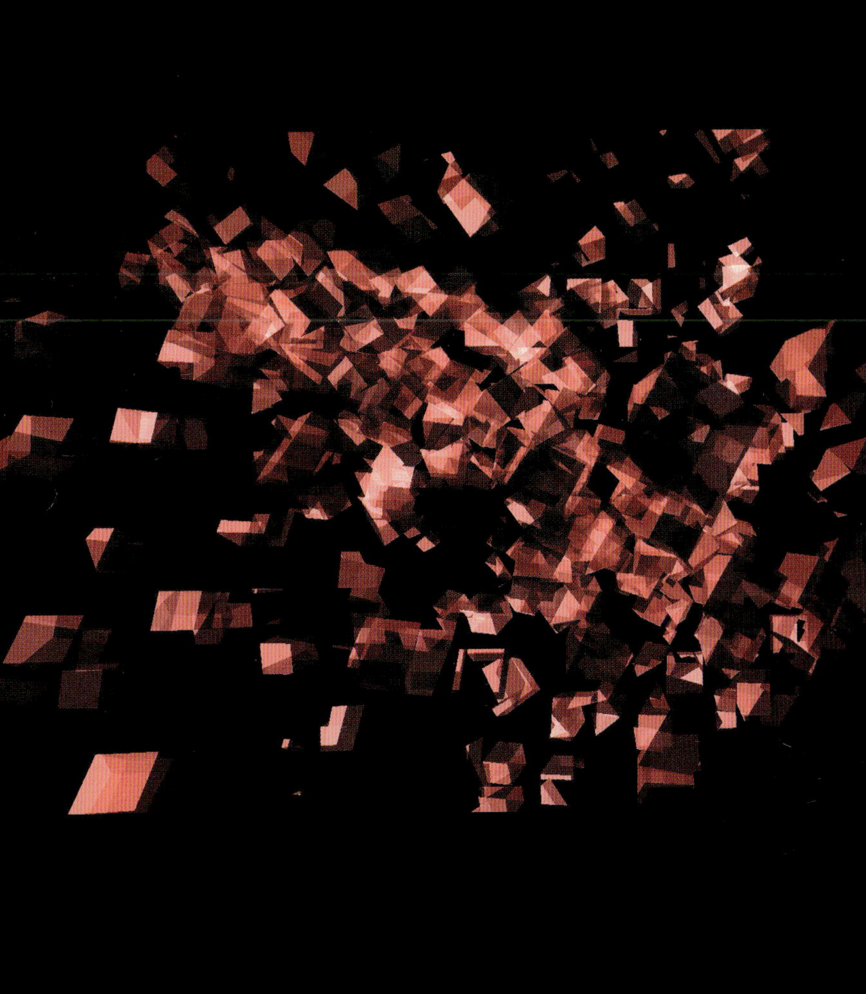

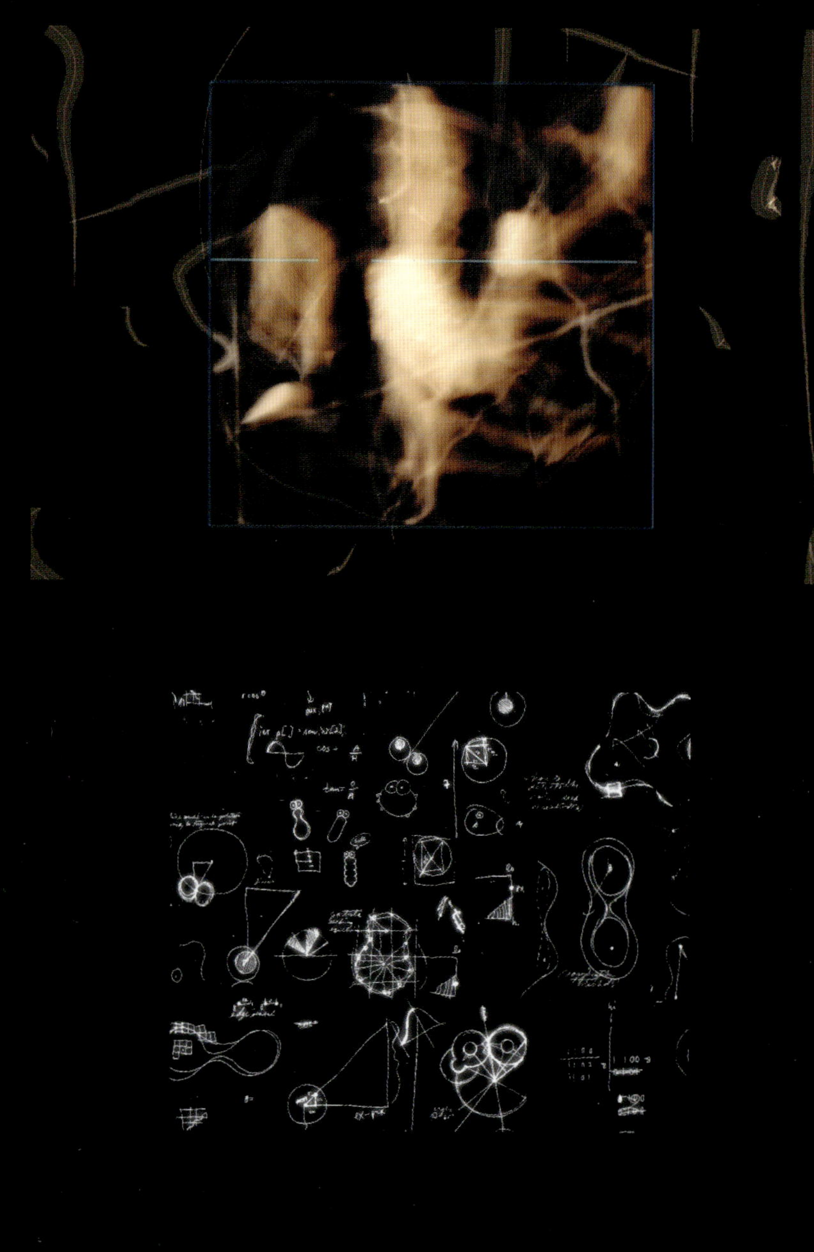

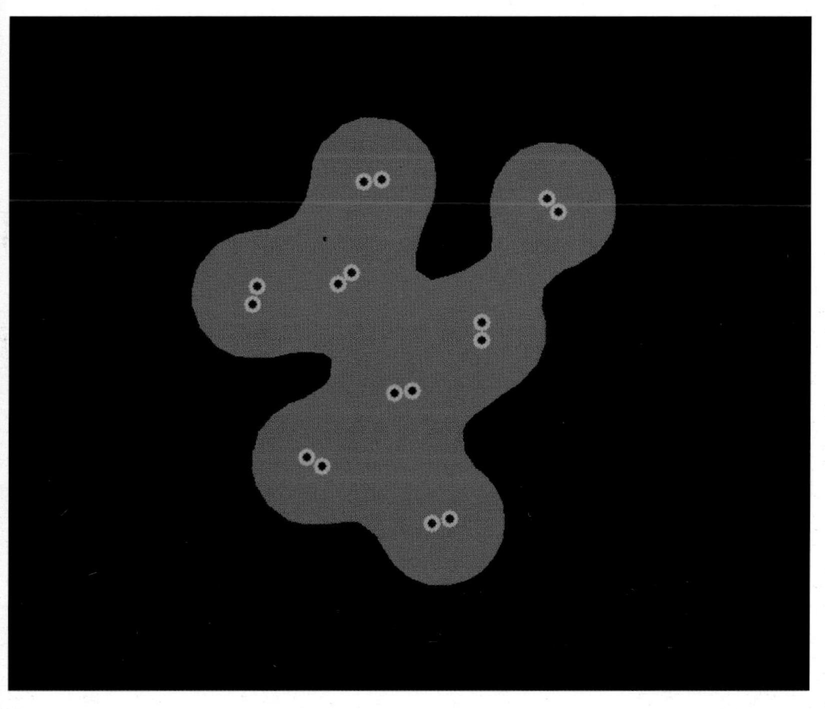

P63 “SPLAT”

SPLAT是互动软件，可让用者创造一组亲切有生气的图形。

P63 "Splat"

Splat is an interactive applet which allows a user to create a group of friendly animating blobs.

## 凯瑟·雷斯

凯瑟·雷斯是在ACG攻读硕士学位的一年级学生，在平面设计方面涉足广泛。一九九六年获得辛辛那提大学设计专业学士学位后，凯瑟在I0/360和RAREMEDIUM工作室任设计总监。他获得的奖项包括美国平面艺术研究院、艺术指导俱乐部及美国设计中心颁发的奖项；他的作品刊登在《ID》、《传递艺术》、《印刷》、《意念》、《艺术论坛》、《FUSE 98》刊物上及在美国平面艺术研究院传递平面展中展出。

Casey Reas is a first-year Master's student in the ACG with an extensive background in graphic design. After receiving a Bachelor's degree in Design from the University of Cincinnati in 1996, Casey served as the Design Director of the i0/360 and RareMedium studios. Casey has won awards from the American Institute of Graphic Arts, Art Directors Club, and American Center for Design; his work has been published or exhibited in ID Magazine, Communication Arts, Print, Idea (Japan), Art Forum, Fuse98, and the AIGA Communication Graphics Show.

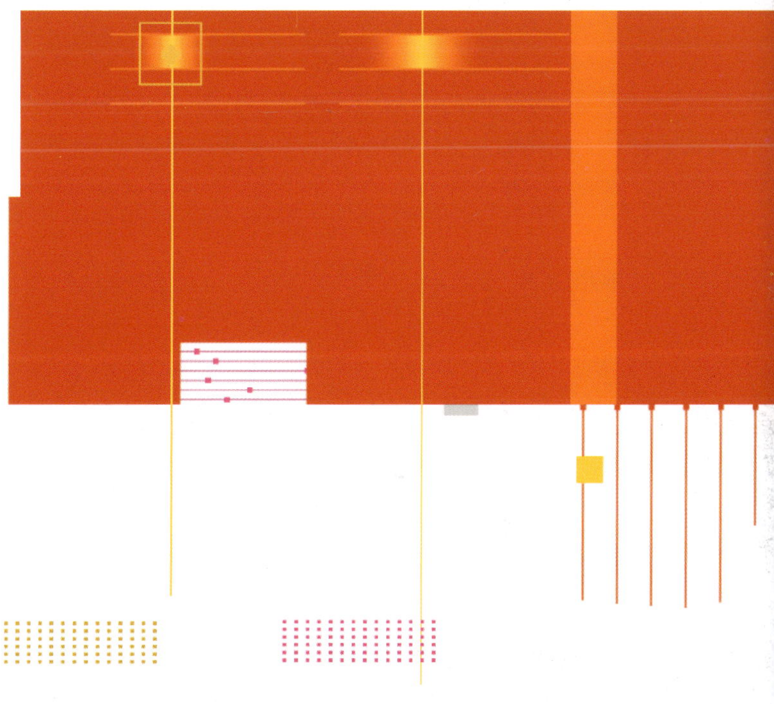

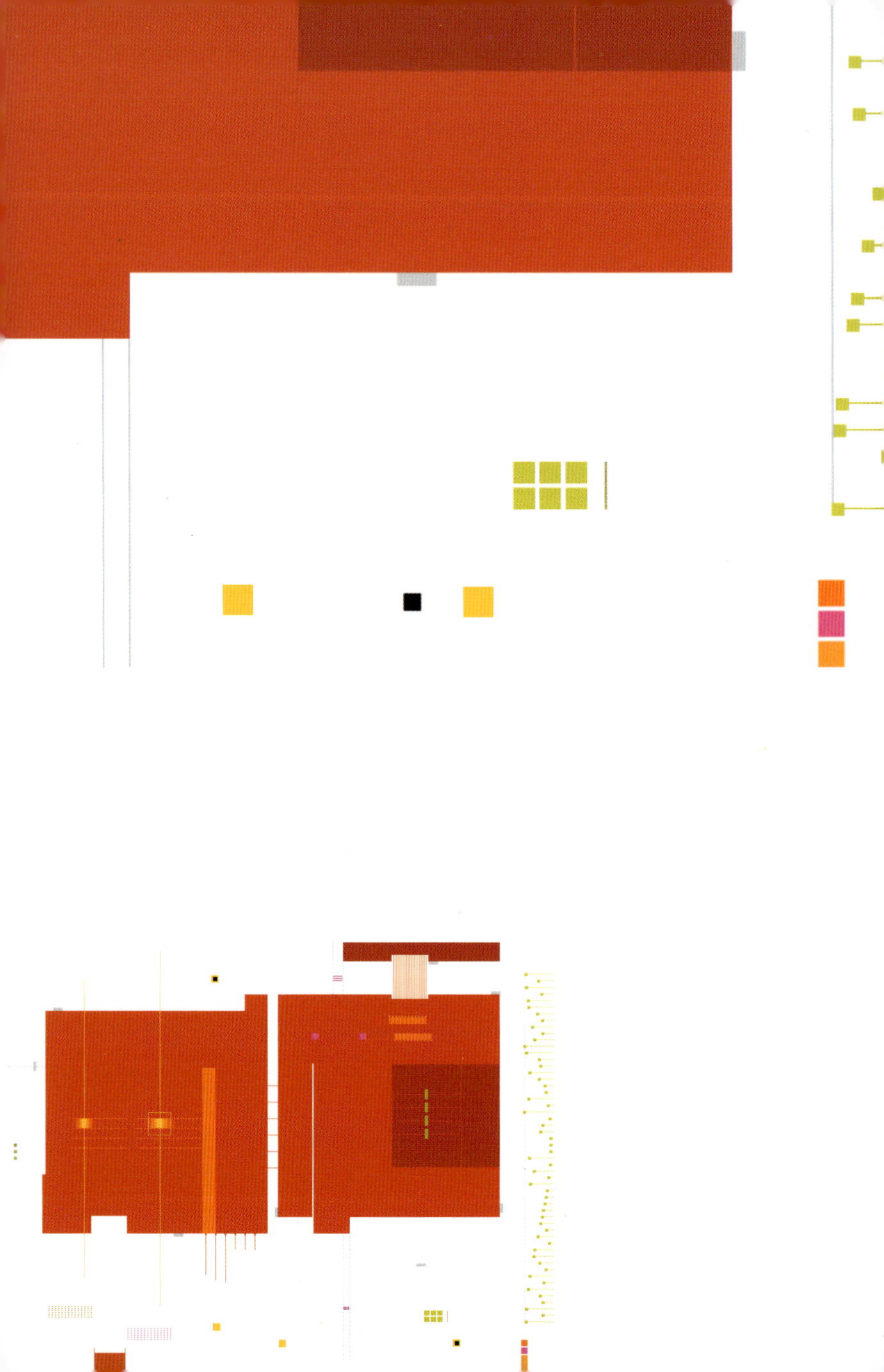

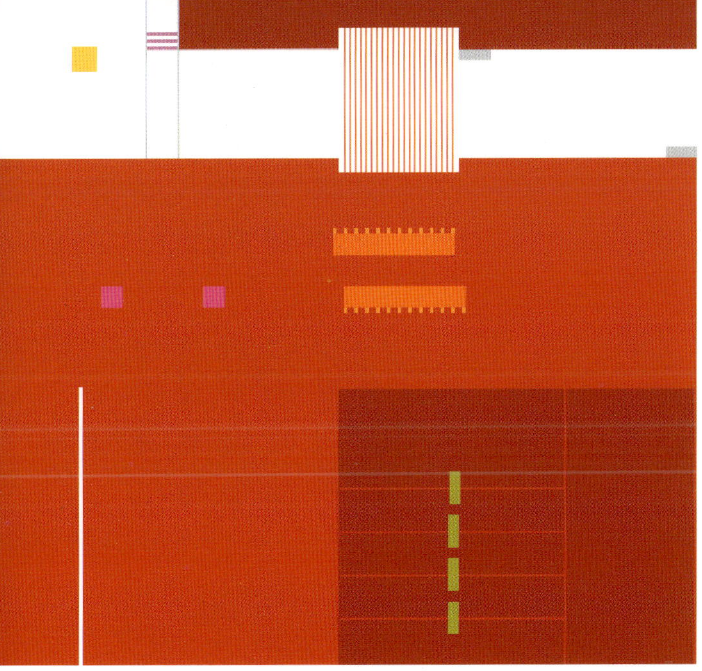

P65-67 "蛋机"

蛋机是一种互动视听系统，一种把视觉关系处理成声音的机器，有意识的操作要求对系统的视觉语言解码，通过处理元素及发展关系，画面的声音输出就可以控制。

P65-67 "Egg Machine"

Egg Machine is an interactive audiovisual system. A machine for processing visual relationships into sound where intentional operation requires decoding the visual language of the system. Through manipulating the elements and creating relationships, the sound output of the image is controlled.

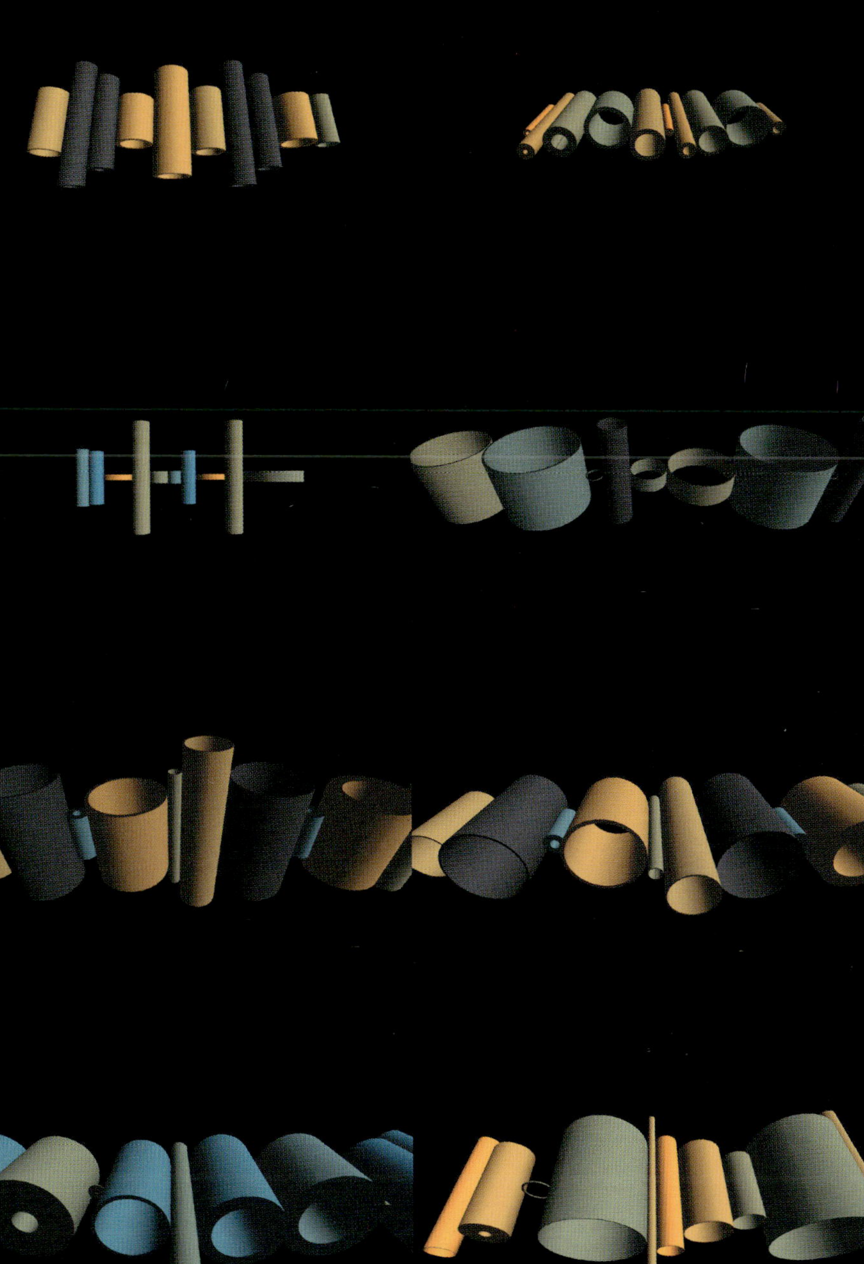

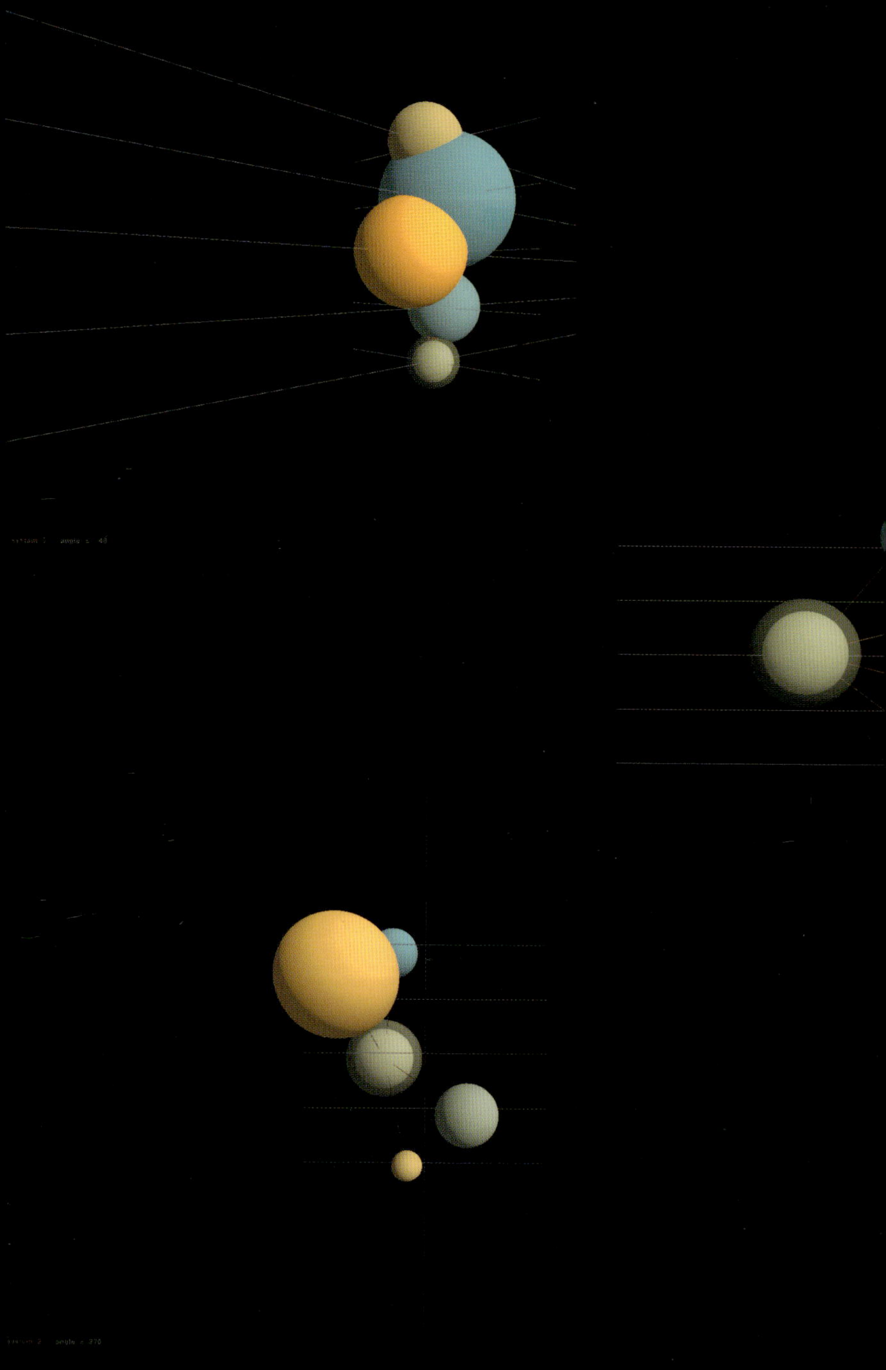
system 1 angle = 48
system 2 angle = 370

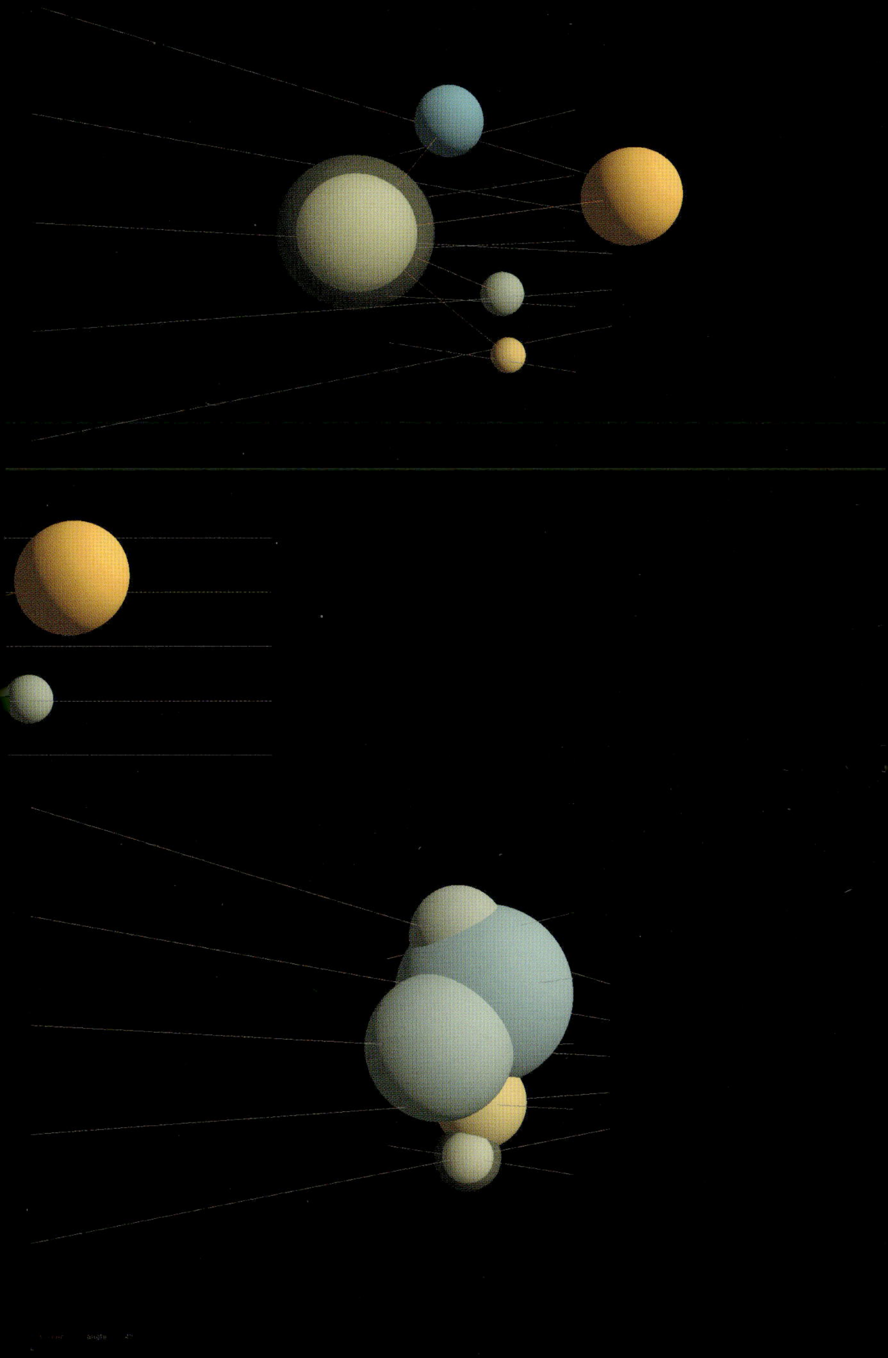
angle

P68-69 "平面调节器"

平面调节器是一个对时间、运动及空间之间的关系分析与实验的系统。对位置、时间及相同物体的多种情形下正片的操作可产生不同的新图形与联系。

P68-69 "Plane Modulator"

The Plane Modulator is a system for analyzing and experiencing the relationships between time, motion, and space. Manipulation of the location, phase, and transparency of multiple instances of the same object creates new forms and connections.

P70-73 "关系结构"

什么是生动组合的美学与经验的可行性，其组合元素了解自己及它们与其它元素的关系？例如，如果组合是稳定的，如何忽视外部的刺激因素而保持平衡关系？如果每个元素知道本身的视觉属性，如何基于以前的与先前输入系统的数据变化它们？

"关系结构"项目专注于这种系统的创新，把定义这些因素的关系视觉化。这是由三个部份组成的系统，原始数据，定义系统的可变视觉展示以及输入系统的数据结果。

P70-73 "Relational Constructs"

What are the aesthetic and experiential possibilities for dynamic compositions whose elements have an understanding of themselves and their relationship to the other elements? For example, what if the composition was homeostatic, constantly trying to maintain equilibrium regardless of external stimulus or if each element knew its visual properties and how to change them based on the past and previous data input into the system.

The Relational Constructs project focuses on the creation of such systems and visualizing the relations that define them. It is a tripartite system composed of raw data, a malleable visual display which defines the system, and the result of the data being fed into the system.

P74 "范围"

在为一种电子程序建立"自己酿造"的电脑后，凯瑟就打算添加A/D硬件及为示波器上的互动处理图形书写一些组合密码。

P74 Scope

After building a 'home brew' computer for an electronics course, Casey was intent on adding A/D hardware and writing some assembly code for interactively processing graphics on an oscilloscope.

P77 "DAKADAKA"（这个项目及全部图像都是和戈兰·莱温共同合作研制的）

打字是一种敲击的空间动作，通过手指的持续节奏来操作。DAKADAKA是一种互动系统，通过定位字体系统与抽象视觉展示的结合来探索打字的程序。

P77 "Dakadaka" (this project and all images are in collaboration with Golan Levin)

Typing is a percussive spatial action, speech spoken through the fingers with continuous rhythms. dakadaka is an interactive system exploring the process of typing by combining positional typographic systems and abstract visual display.

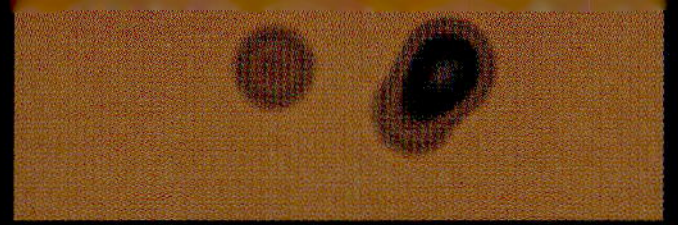
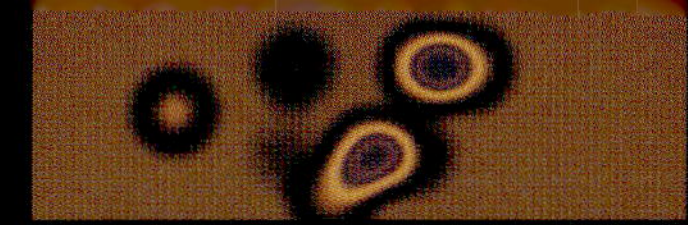

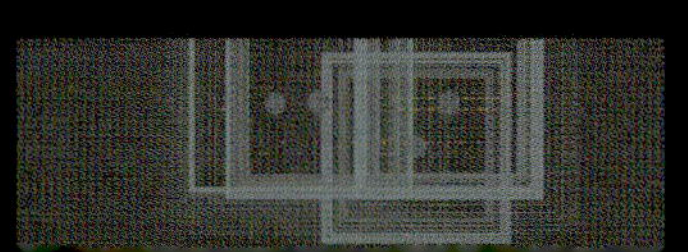
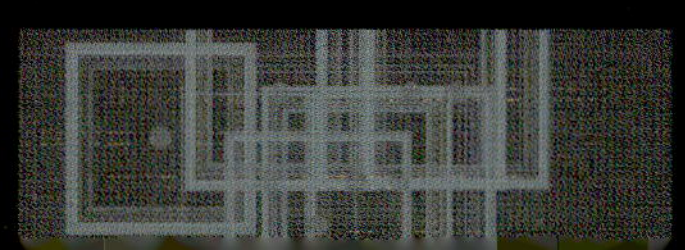

## 杰雷・舒夫曼

杰雷・舒夫曼是在ACG攻读硕士学位的一年级学生，他的兴趣是运用电脑作为一种视觉媒体及工具，为观看和控制信息与程序而创造新方式。在麻省理工学院攻读电脑科学学士学位时，杰雷编写了CLAYSCAPE 3D软件，一种流行的三维模型直观软件。

Jared Schiffman is a first-year Master's student in the ACG, interested in using the computer as a visual medium and as tool to create new methods for viewing and manipulating both information and processes. While working on an undergraduate degree in Computer Science at MIT, Jared created ClayScape3D, a popular shareware package for intuitive 3D modelling.

杰雷研究的焦点是使程序对视觉艺术家而言更容易掌握。最近他做了几个环境程序的实验草图，显示了电脑的可视部分，如电脑工作的流程，以及存储器的操作（作品创作时间均为1999-2000）。

The focus of Jared research is making the task of programming more accessible to the visual artist. Recently, he has done several experimental sketches for a programming environment which manifests the invisible aspects of computation, such as the flow of the computational process, and the manipulation of memory.

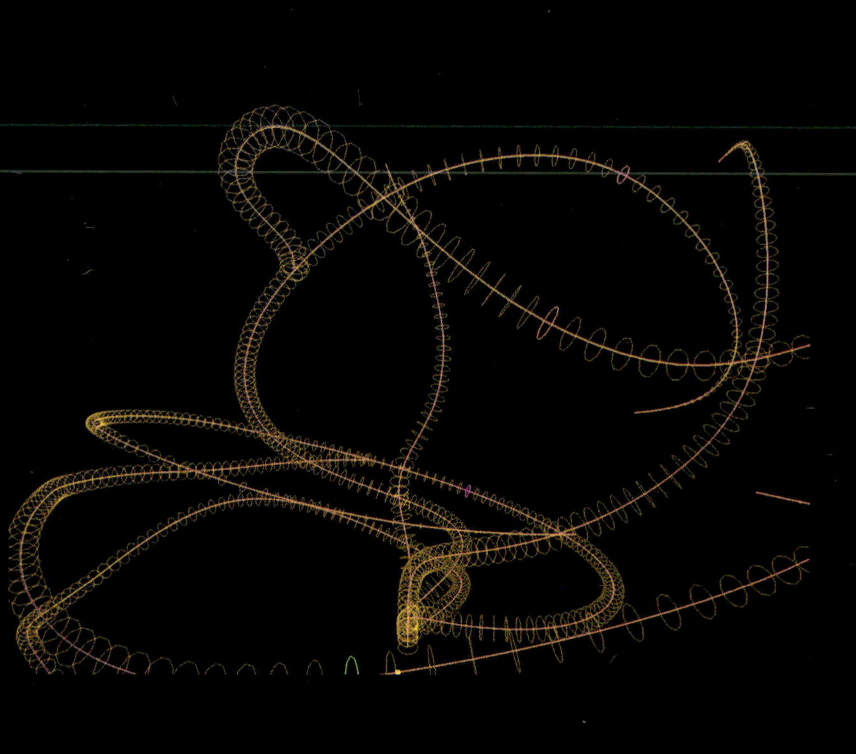

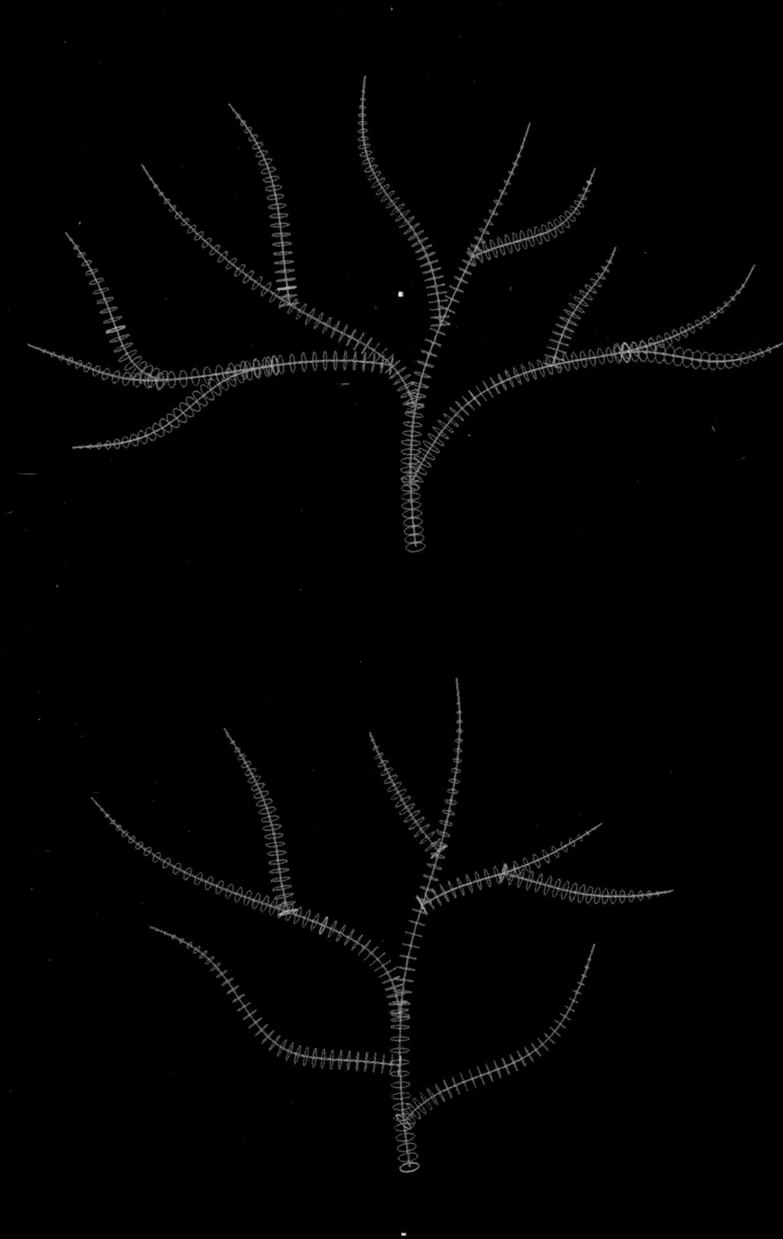

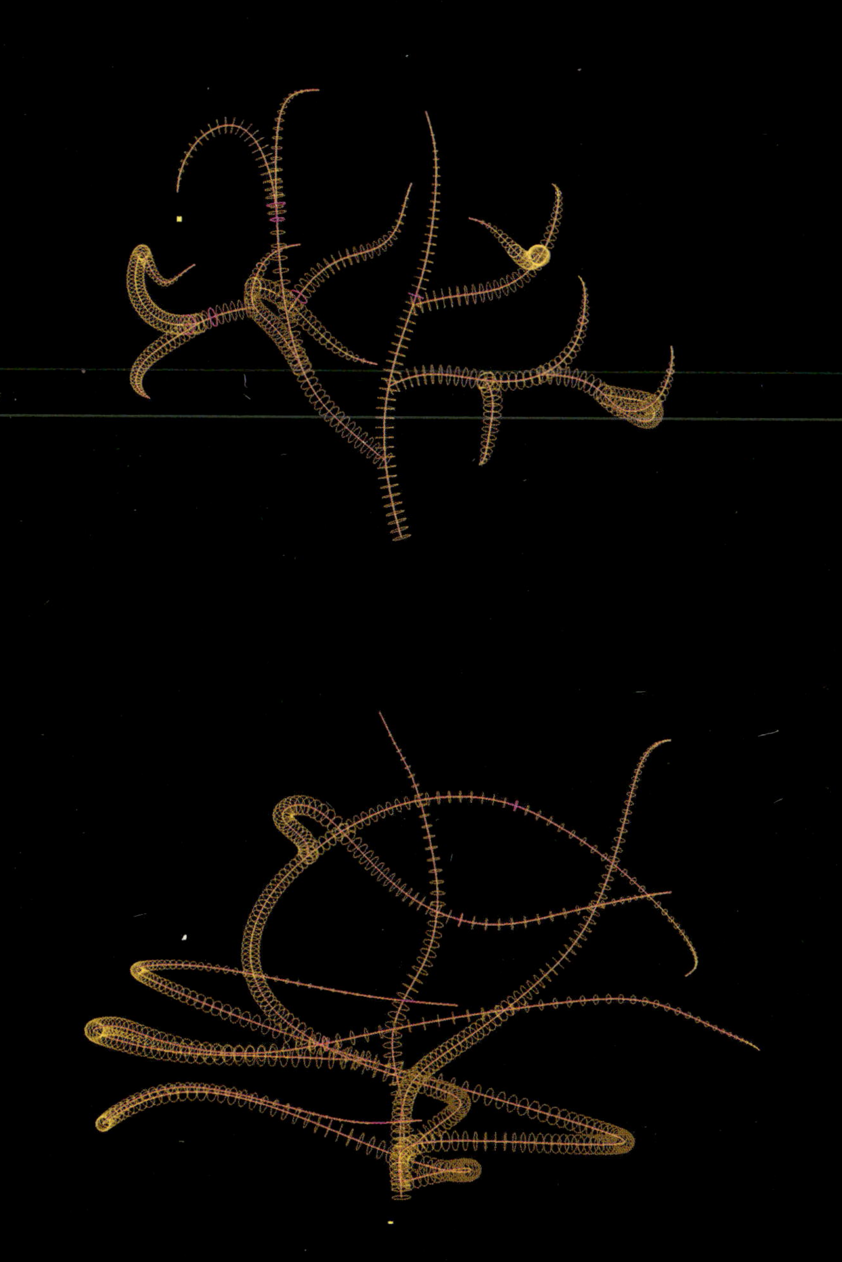

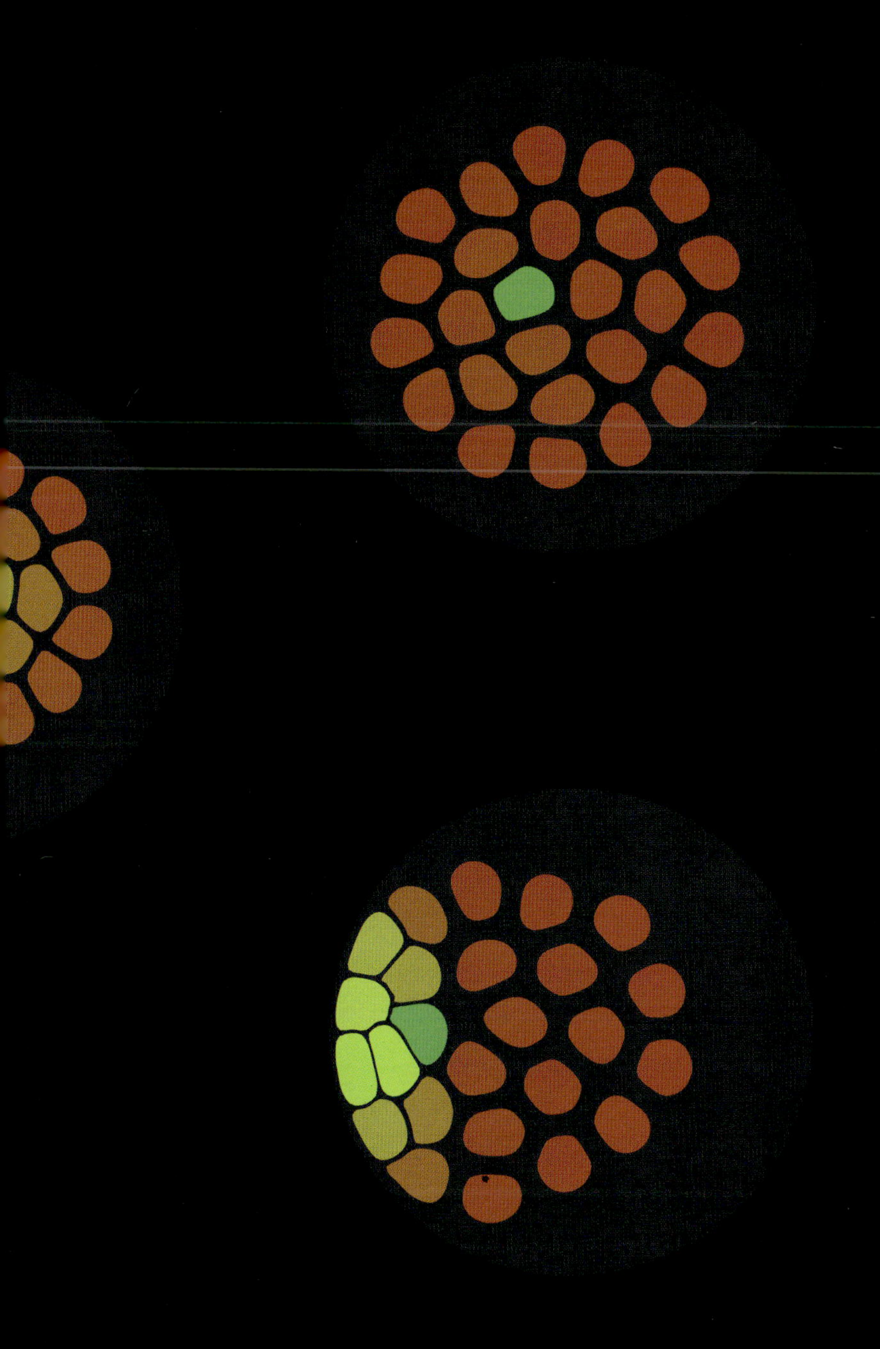

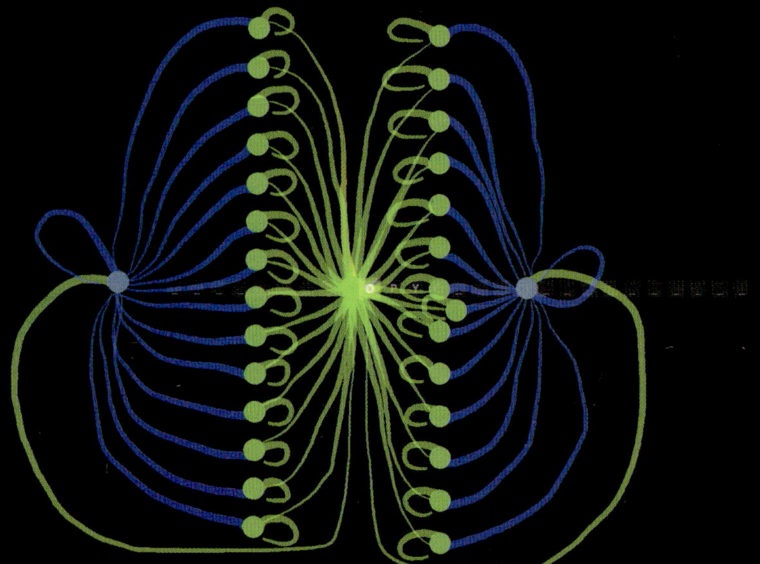

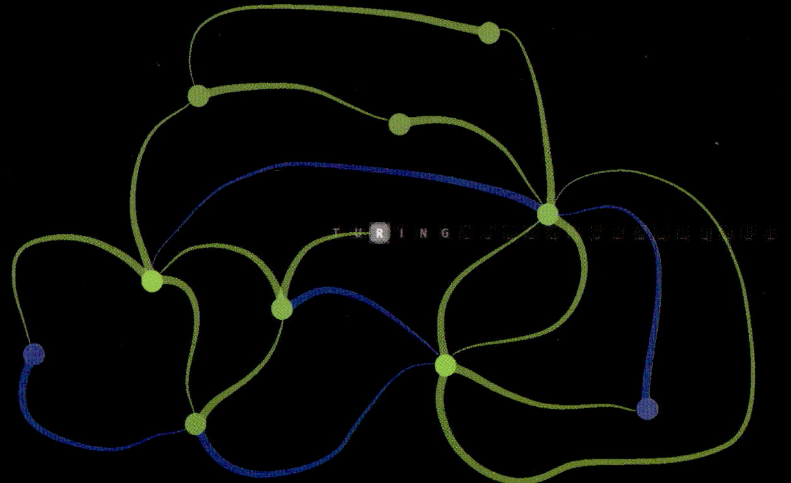
TURING

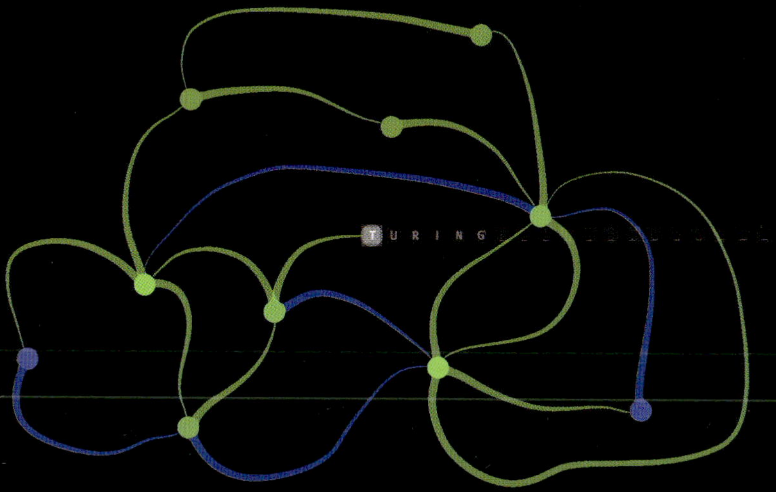

TURING

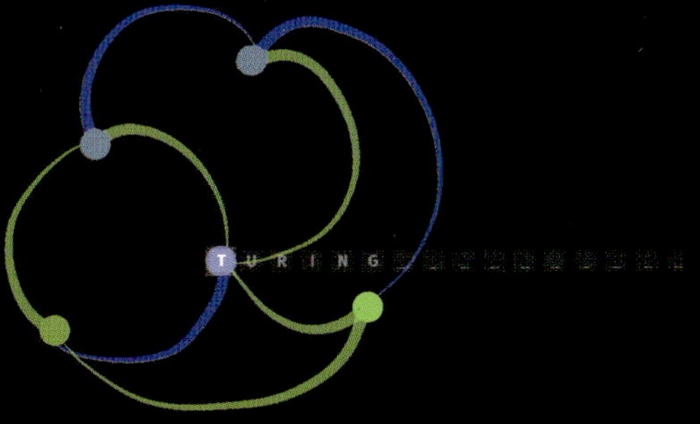

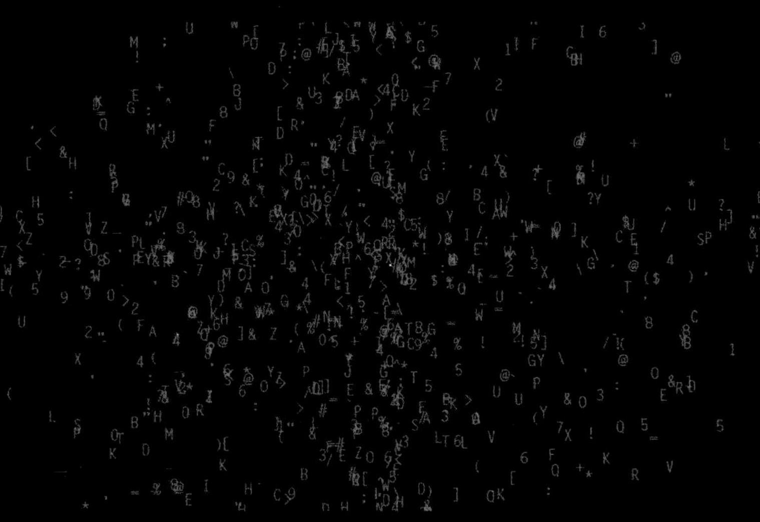

mytest

```
#include "acApp.h"
#include "acu.h"
#include "Buffer.h"
#include "Button.h"

class coderApp : public acApp
{
public:
  coderApp();

  void Draw();
  void HandleKey( char C, int x, int y );
  void HandleMouse( int button, int state, int x, int y );

  void HandleMotion( int x, int y );
  void HandleSpecialKey( int key, int x, int y );

  void AddBuffer( Buffer* newBuffer );

#define MAX_NUM_BUFFERS 256
  Buffer* B[ MAX_NUM_BUFFERS ];
  int numBuffers;
  boolean MouseIsDown;

  Button* fullScreenButton;
```

cap

app.C

```
#include "acApp.h"
#include "acu.h"
#include "Buffer.h"
#include "Button.h"

class coderApp : public acApp
{
public:
  coderApp();

  void Draw();
  void HandleKey( char C, int x, int y );
  void HandleMouse( int button, int state, int x, int y );
  void HandleMotion( int x, int y );
  void HandleSpecialKey( int key, int x, int y );

  void AddBuffer( Buffer* newBuffer );

#define MAX_NUM_BUFFERS 256
  Buffer* B[ MAX_NUM_BUFFERS ];
  int numBuffers;
  boolean MouseIsDown;

  Button* fullScreenButton;
  boolean isFullScreen;
  Button* newBufferButton;
};
```

snapst

```
#define MAX_NUM_BUFFERS 256
  Buffer* B[ MAX_NUM_BUFFERS ];
  int numBuffers;
  boolean MouseIsDown;
```

P79-81 "GROWGRAM"

GROWGRAM是为三维系统作的草图，在该系统中，用者绘出一些各种程序可效仿的轨迹。圆环代表单个编码线，岔开的分支表示条件叙述。最终，用者可在每一分支如乘过山车一样首先观察过程。

P79-81 "Growgram"

Growgram is a sketch for a 3D system in which the user would draw paths which represent the various paths that the program may follow. The rings represent individual lines of code, and the diverging branches represent conditional statements. Ultimately, the user may take a first person view of the process, by riding inside each branch like a roller coaster.

P82-83 "蜂蜜"

蜂蜜与以上的研究没有联系。蜂蜜的目的是试图创造一个真正的有机几何图案，像圆圈或方形，除了这种新图案具有易变的形状外，它还会在显示器上与其它邻居相互作用。每个图案总维持在其原有的范围，绝不会在任何位置伸展得太细。在实施过程中，图案如物体局限于一个鱼缸中，活动受到限制。

P82-83 "Honey"

Honey is unrelated to the above research. The purpose of Honey was to try to create a truly organic geometric primitive, like a circle, or square, except that this new primitive would have a malleable shape, and would interact with its on screen neighbors. Each primitive always maintains its original area, and never stretches too thin in any one place. In this implementation, the primitives are trapped in a kind of fish bowl like object which limits their movement.

P84-85 "图宁"

第一张"图宁"草图是基于著名的二战时代电脑科学家艾伦·图宁创造的简单电脑模型。在这个程序中，每一条粗线就是一条精确的编码线。图宁将电脑操作者（连接网）与记忆融入一个整体空间，最终的效果如在原始材料上工作的一部强有力机器。

P84-85 "Turing"

The first of these sketches, Turing, is based on simple model of computation created by Alan Turing, the famous WWII era computer scientist. In this program, each thick line is literally a line of code. Turing merges the computational operators (the net of connections) and the memory being manipulated (the line of characters) into a unified space, so that end result is an impression of a powerful machine working on a raw material.

## 艾里斯·科

艾里斯·科是在ACG攻读硕士学位的二年级学生。于一九九八年获得麻省理工学院建筑与电脑科学学士学位。

她目前专注于时装与人体关系间的技术与电脑的探索。

Elise Co is a second-year Master's student in the ACG. Elise received a Bachelor's degree in Architecture and Computer Science from MIT in 1998.

Her present focus is on the exploration of technology and computation in the context of fashion and the body.

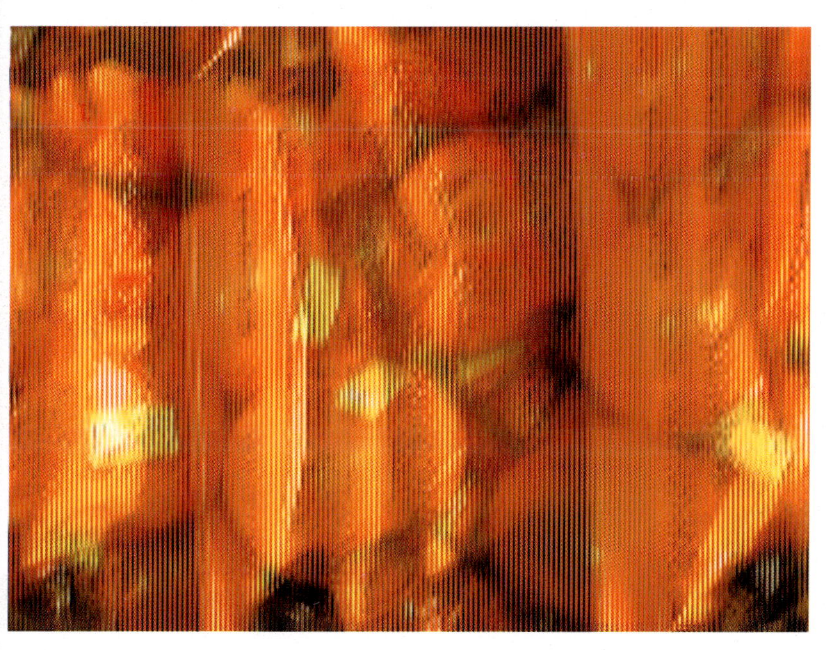

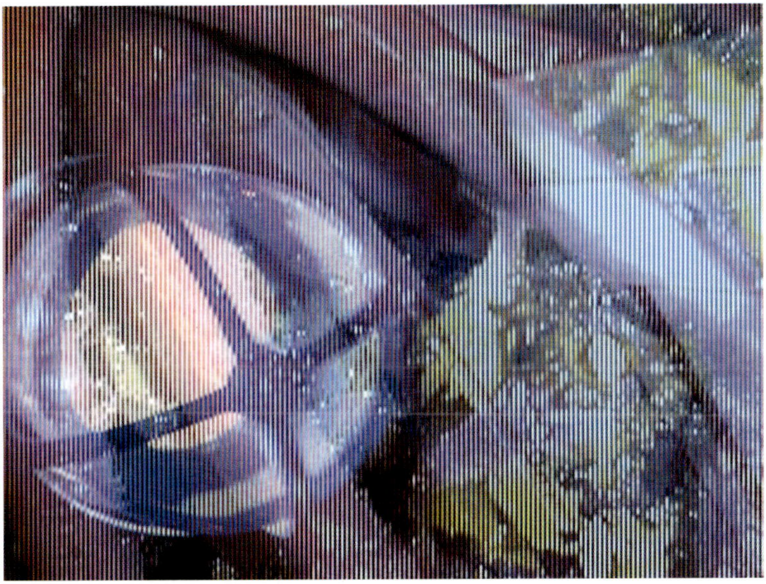

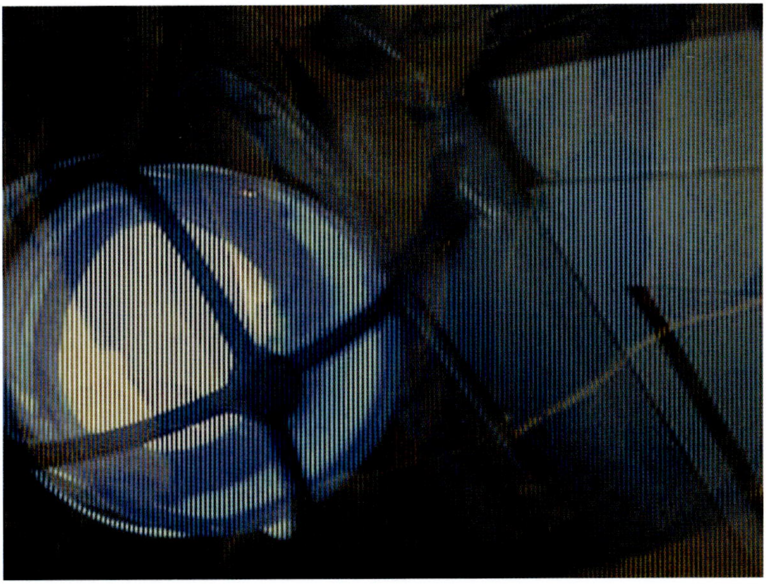

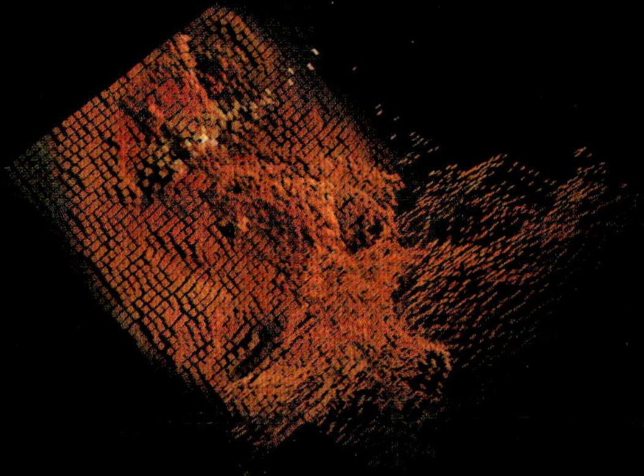

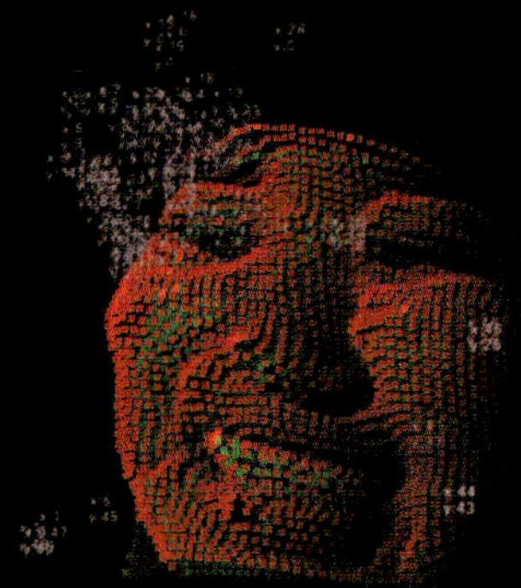

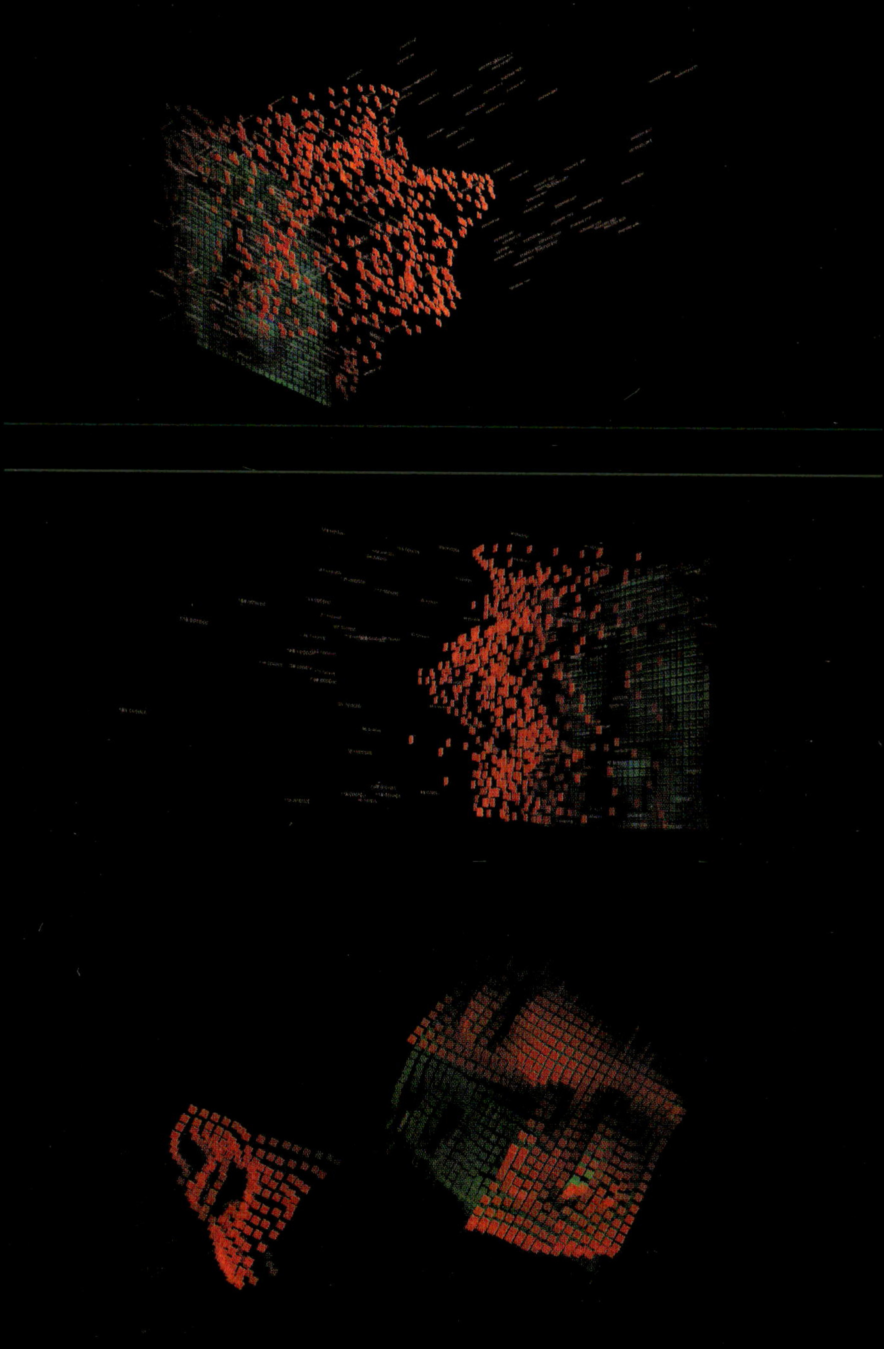

# 汤姆·怀特

汤姆·怀特是麻省理工学院媒体实验室的研究助理，在约翰·梅达教授指导下的ACG小组工作。ACG小组专注于探索电脑科学与平面设计之间的自然交叠。汤姆过去的工作着重于以电脑媒介——通常是采用新硬件的设计来创造新的传递方式。他的硕士论文以LIQUID HAPTICS新界面为研究重点。最近，汤姆以攻读博士学位的身份在实验室研究一种新软件系统，该系统是作为展示、构成并与复杂异步电脑互动的软件。

Tom White is a research assistant at the MIT Media Laboratory, working in the Aesthetics and Computation group under professor John Maeda. This group focuses on exploring the natural intersection between the disciplines of computer science and graphic design. Tom's past work focused on creating new ways of communicating with computational media, often through the design of new hardware devices. His masters thesis centered on a new family of interfaces known as Liquid Haptics. Currently a PhD candidate at the lab, Tom is working on a new software system for representing, constructing, and interacting with complex asynchronous computation.

P95 "TW-VID"
TW-VID一种影视的相互作用，其中摄影机将形象转换成一系列的线条。这一特定的形象是汤姆举起手臂的图象，你可以作出躯干、头与手臂的画面。

P95 "TW-VID"
TW-VID a video interaction in which a camera transforms an image into a series of lines. This particular image is a picture of Tom's holding up an arm - and you can just make out the torso, head, and arm.

P96 "TW-BOOK"
TW-BOOK是为比尔·米歇尔设计的一本书籍封面的形象，由汤姆与大卫·西摩尔设计。字体在向量场上浮动，量场是一种旋涡的物理模仿。

P96 "TW-BOOK"
This is an image designed for a book cover designed by Tom and David Small for Bill Mitchell. The words are flowing in a vector field which is a physical simulation of a vortex.

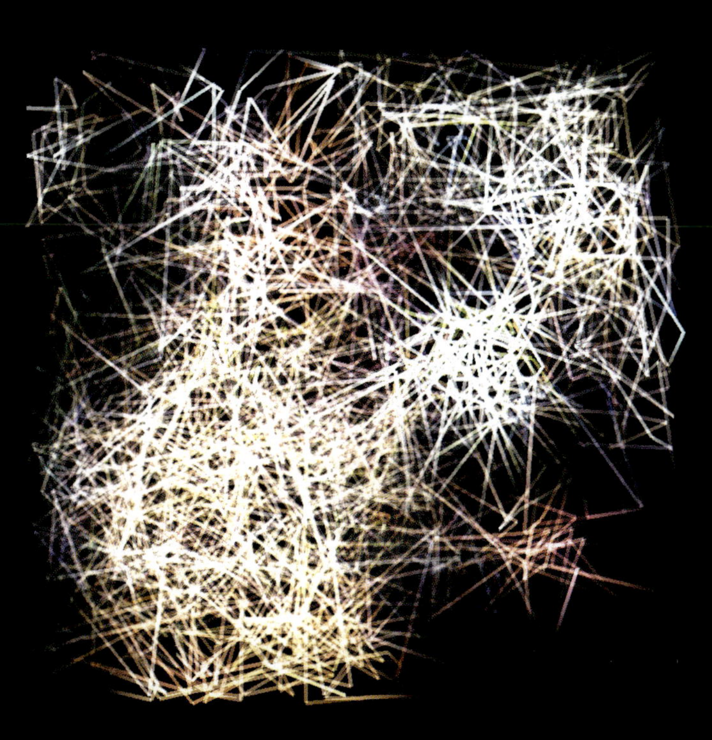

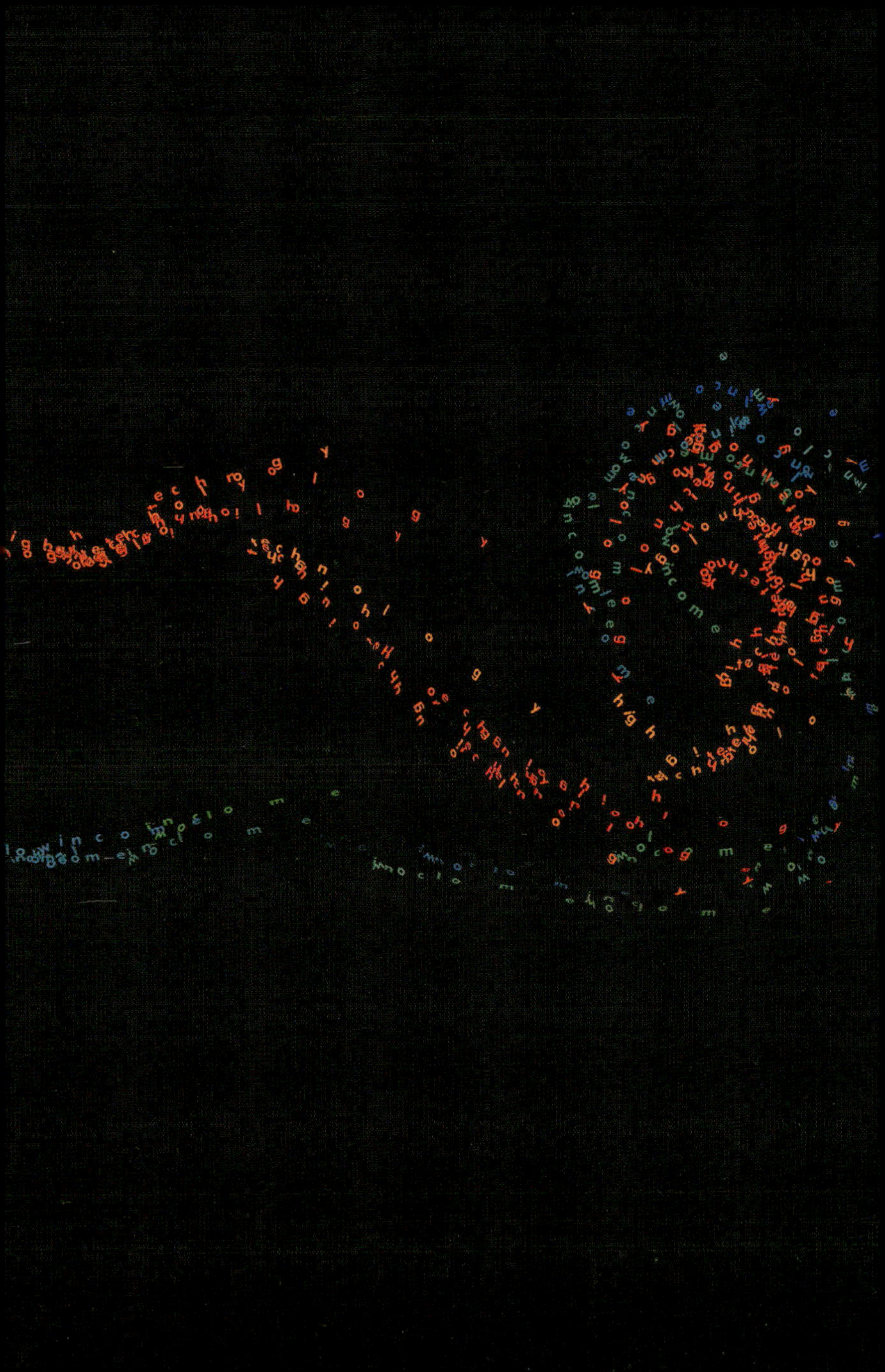

ideas
generate
your
mind
horizons
goes on
of

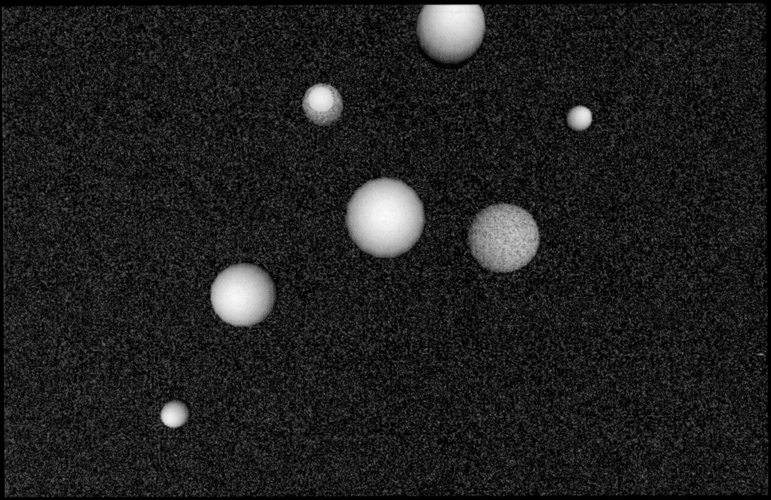

P97 "TW-SOM"

TW-SOM，河流或意识流，是一个由汤姆与同学大卫·西摩尔构思与实施的大型互动装置。装置位于约六平方英尺的小花园，花园中是流动的水，水上有一些字。花园边的流体可让人通过推、挠与流动的字体相互作用。如果直接压在字体上，字体将会胀大，爆裂成一些相关的文字，文字继续在水中流动。

P97 "TW-SOM"

TW-SOM, Stream, or Stream of Consciousness, was a large interactive installation conceived and implemented by Tom and fellow student David Small. The piece centers around a small garden, roughly six feet square. In the garden is flowing water, and in the water flows a handful of words. A liquid pad to the side of the garden allows people to interact with the words flowing by, pushing and stirring them. If someone presses directly on a word, it will swell and explode into a handful of related words, which will continue to flow through the water.

P98 "TW-BUB"

这是二维与三维结合的实验性视觉空间的画面。相似的二维象数平面是透明的，三维物体可在此平面前后移动。

"TW-KITE"

该项目是约翰·梅达的视觉界面设计课程的一部分，时间为一星期。在这个项目中，约翰简单地要求学生设计一个能以鼠标控制飞行的风筝，其界面是明显的、黑白的。JAVA应用程序的结果是一个飞行风筝的抽象图象，鼠标让一个人在地面上移动，试图让风筝起飞。山丘与风形成黑白的旋涡力，推动风筝离人而去。

P98 "TW-BUB"

This is a screenshot from an experimental visual space that combines two and three dimensions. The familiar two dimensional pixel plane is given transparency and three-dimensional objects can move in front or behind this plane.

"TW-KITE"

This program was part of a one-week assignment in John Maeda's Principles of Visual Interface Design course. In this assignment, John simply asked students to make a kite that you could fly with your mouse, where the interface was self-evident and monochrome. The java application that resulted is an abstraction of kite flying, with the mouse moving a person across a terrain trying to get his kite to fly. The hills and wind are both merged into a black and white swirling pattern of forces that push the kite away from the person.

P100 "TW-RED"

这个来自涂料程序的画面，是使用汤姆的流体触觉界面方式形成。山丘是汤姆的五个手指压在垫块的结果，色彩则保存在画布上。

"TW-CUBE"

这个小程序也是梅达界面设计课程的一部分，但注意力在于颜色与随意性。

项目的特别部分是创造一个随意的程序，将屏幕分为两半颜色，设计一种电脑性质的视觉效果，从而把两半的颜色联系一起，这方式使颜色的分别不会太大。汤姆的方法是将两种分离的颜色处理成一个二维平面的两半，创造一个数学上连结两半的三维立体。

P100 "TW-RED"

A screenshot from a paint program that used Tom's liquid haptic interface device. The five hills are the result of his five fingers pressing on the pad and result in paint being deposited on the canvas.

"TW-CUBE"

This small program was also part of Maeda's Interface Design course, but this particular week the attention was on color and randomness. The assignment for this particular part was to create a random process that would color two halves of the screen along with designing a visual mechanism of computational nature for relating the two halves of color in such a way that the difference in colors is not felt so deeply. Tom's solution was to treat the two disparate colors as two halves of a two dimensional plane, and to create a three dimensional solid that mathematically bridged the two halves.

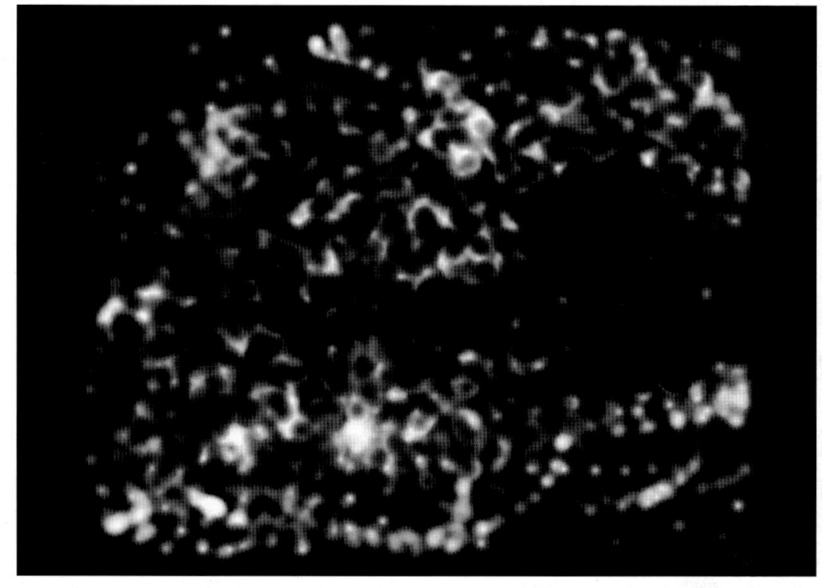

P102 "TW-TALK"

一种实验性的字体，基于英文的四十个音素。无论是否发出声音，说话时字形对应于口形。

"TW-BALL"

这是一种实验性绘画程序的画面。在该程序中，画笔由一组球代替，球绕着一个焦点在三维中绕行，当其中一个球划过画布，笔迹就保存。

P102 "TW-TALK"

An experimental font that was based on the 40 phonemes of English speech. Letterforms correspond to the shape of the mouth when spoken, whether the sound is voiced, and other structural properties of talking.

"TW-BALL"

This is a screenshot from an experimental paint program. In this program, the brush was replaced by a handful of balls orbiting in three dimensions around the focus point, and paint is deposited when one of the balls crosses the canvas.

## 本杰明・佛莱

本杰明・佛莱是在ACG攻读硕士学位的二年级学生。他于一九九七年获得卡耐基梅伦大学设计学院学士学位，其专业是平面设计并副修电脑科学。他专注于将适应性的和有机的信息视觉化。本杰明被《ID》杂志的二零零零年一月刊评为〝三十岁以下的四十位顶尖设计师〞中的一员。

Benjamin Fry is a second-year Master's student in the ACG. Ben received an undergraduate degree in 1997 from the School of Design at Carnegie Mellon University, with a major in Graphic Design and a minor in Computer Science. His focus is on adaptive and organic information visualization.
Ben was named one of the "Top 40 Designers Under 30" by ID Magazine in January 2000.

由本杰明・佛莱设计的作品是基于梅达的数字摄影课程。
APPLET是本杰明色彩绘画程序的新版本，你看到的形象是一个颜色轮（这里是一个方块），其结构源自六种色彩形象而不是纯颜色。每个形象主要是一个原色或次要颜色（红、黄、橙等）。APPLET在不同的形象中插入以便建造轮子。按下鼠标，形象开始活动。移动鼠标可从中心开始旋转轮子。（作品均创作于1999-2000）

Work by Ben Fry, form Maeda's class on numeric photography.
This applet is a new version of Ben's color paint program. The image you see here is a color wheel (or in this case, a square) constructed from six color images instead of pure colors. Each image is predominantly a primary or secondary color (red, yellow, orange, etc.) The applet interpolates between the different images to construct the wheel. Pressing the mouse starts animation in the image. Dragging the mouse 'rotates' the wheel, beginning from the center.

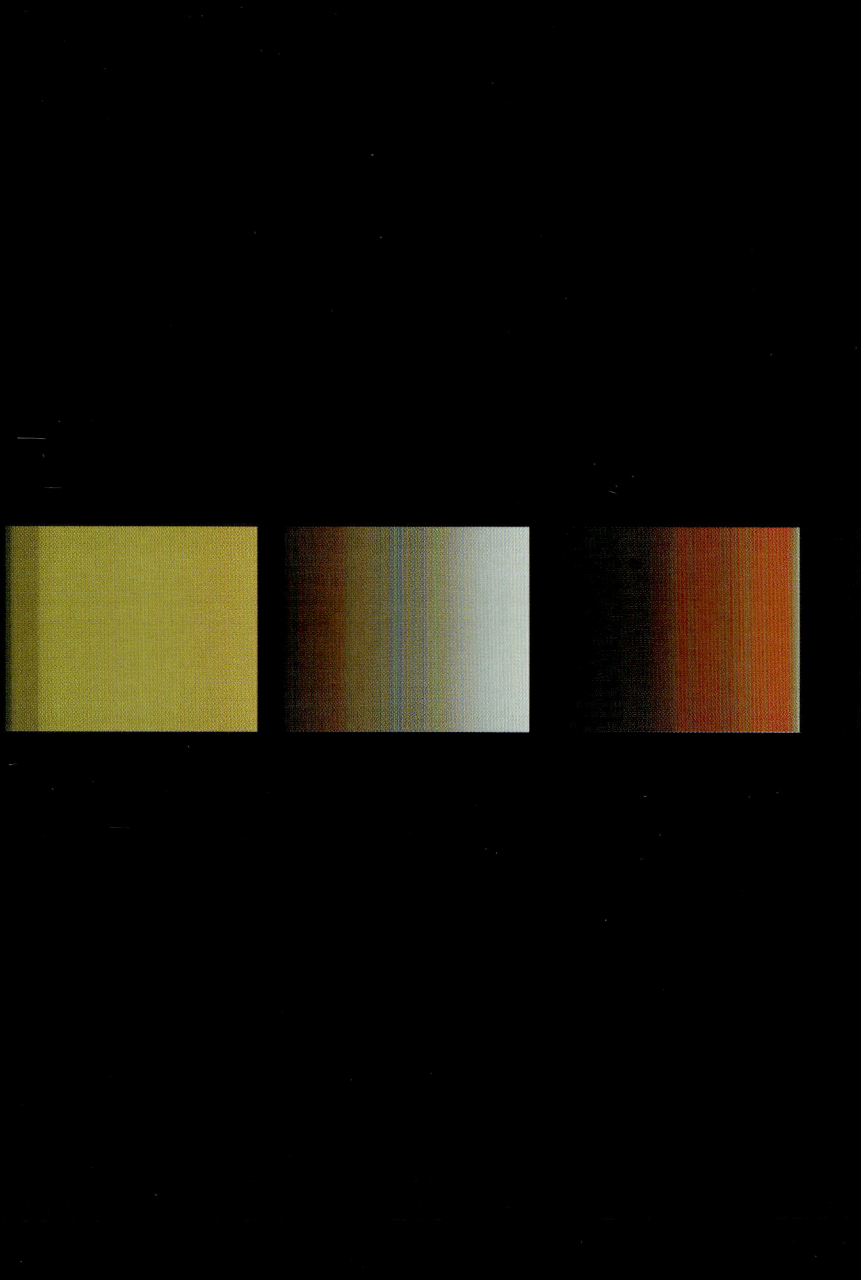

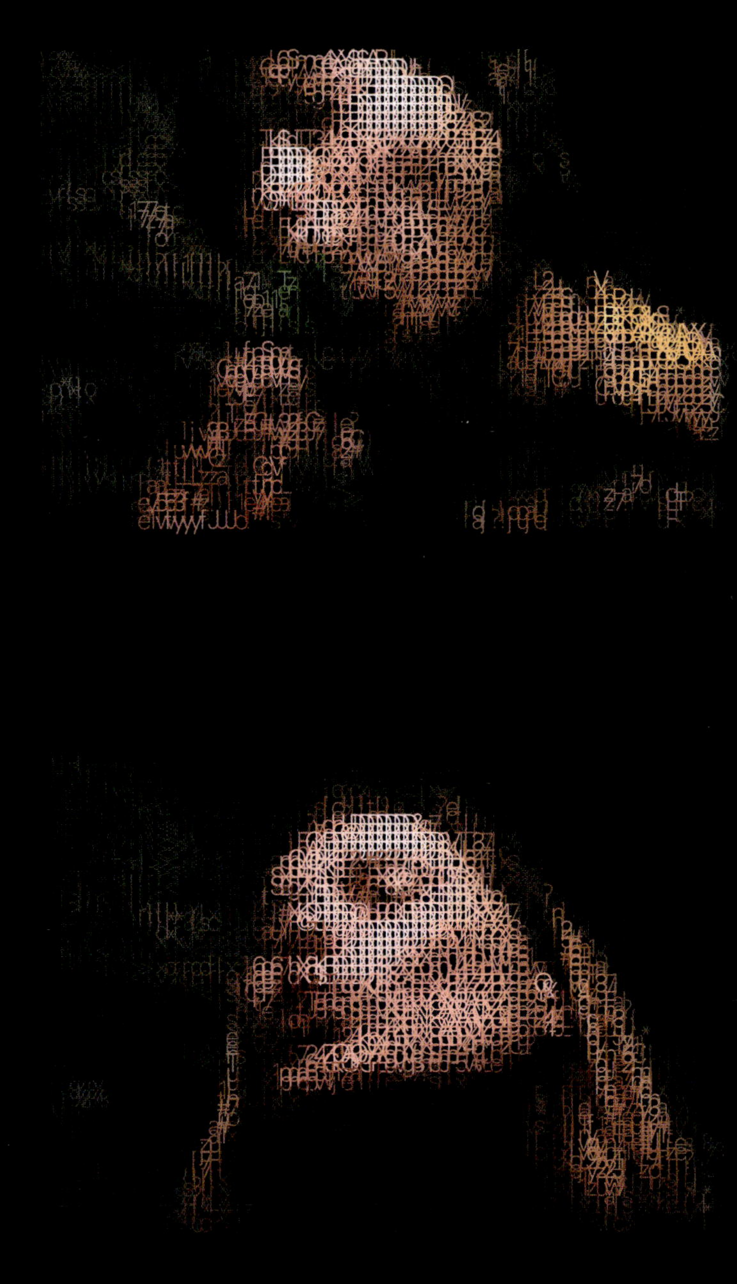

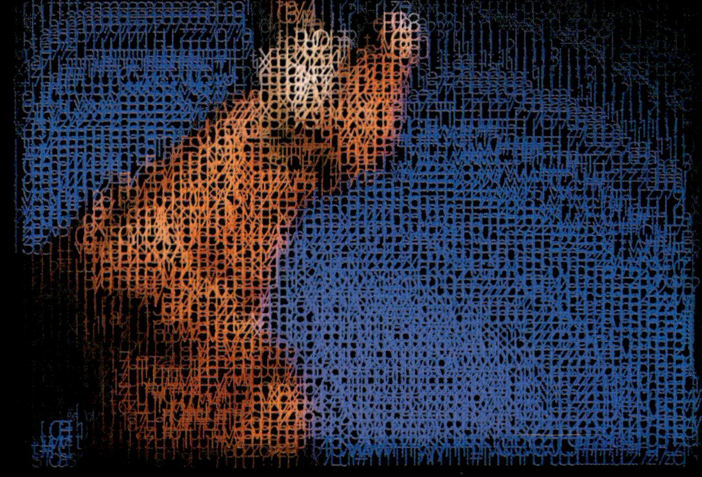

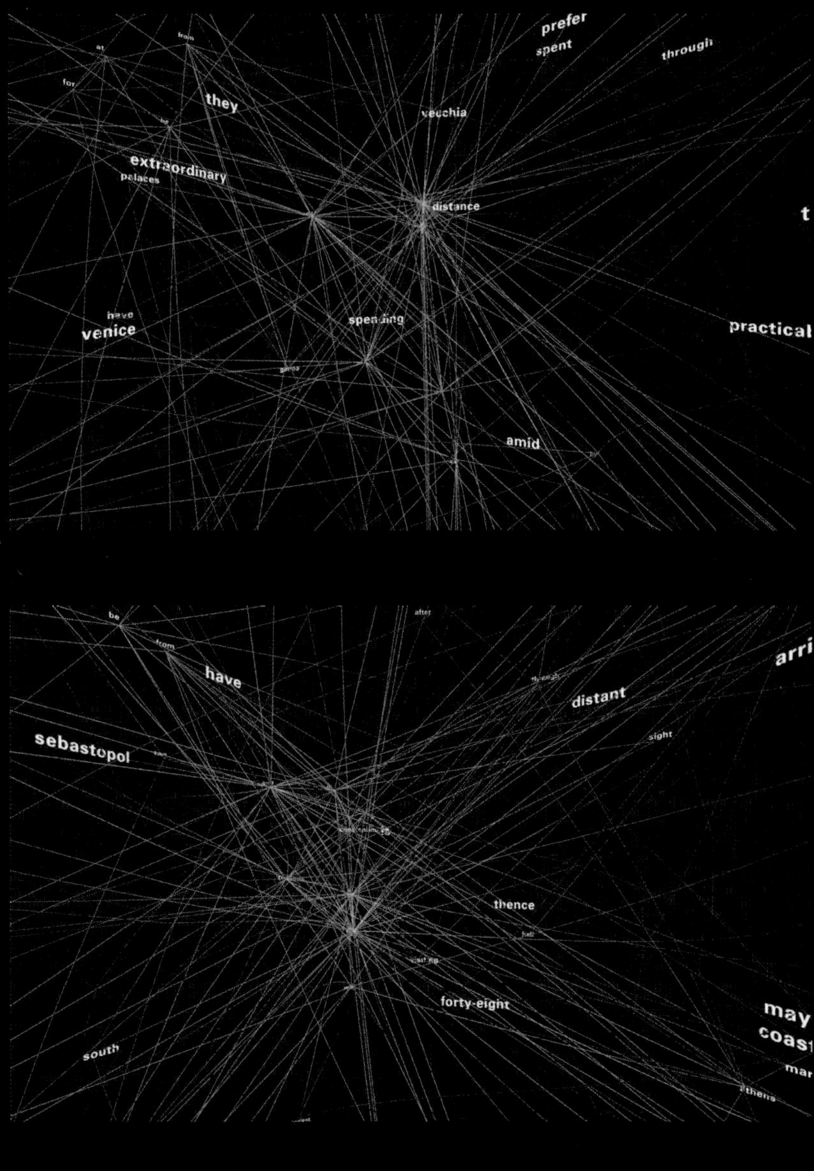

from
at
for
prefer
spent
through
they
vecchia
extraordinary
palaces
distance
have
venice
spending
practical
amid
be
after
from
have
distant
sebastopol
sight
thence
forty-eight
may
south
athens

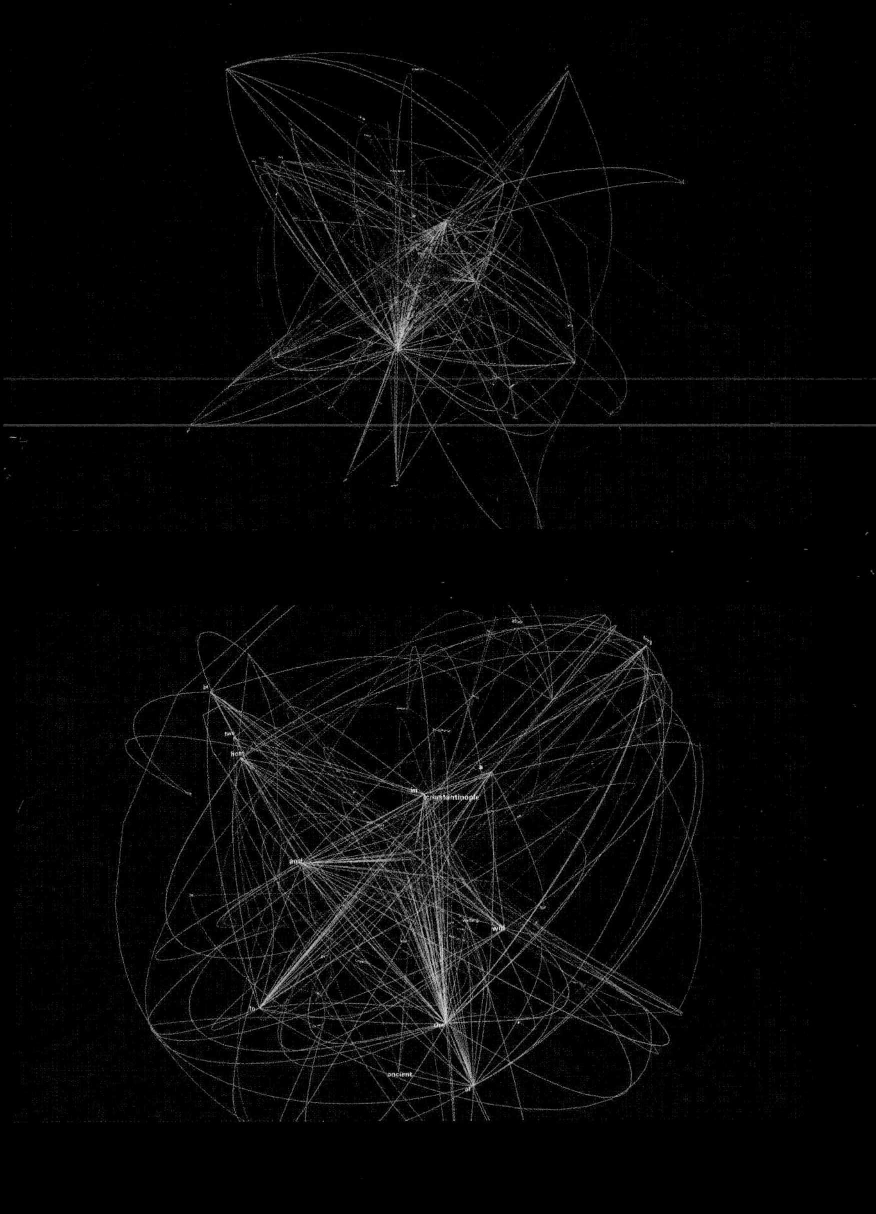

in
constantinople
and
will
to
ancient

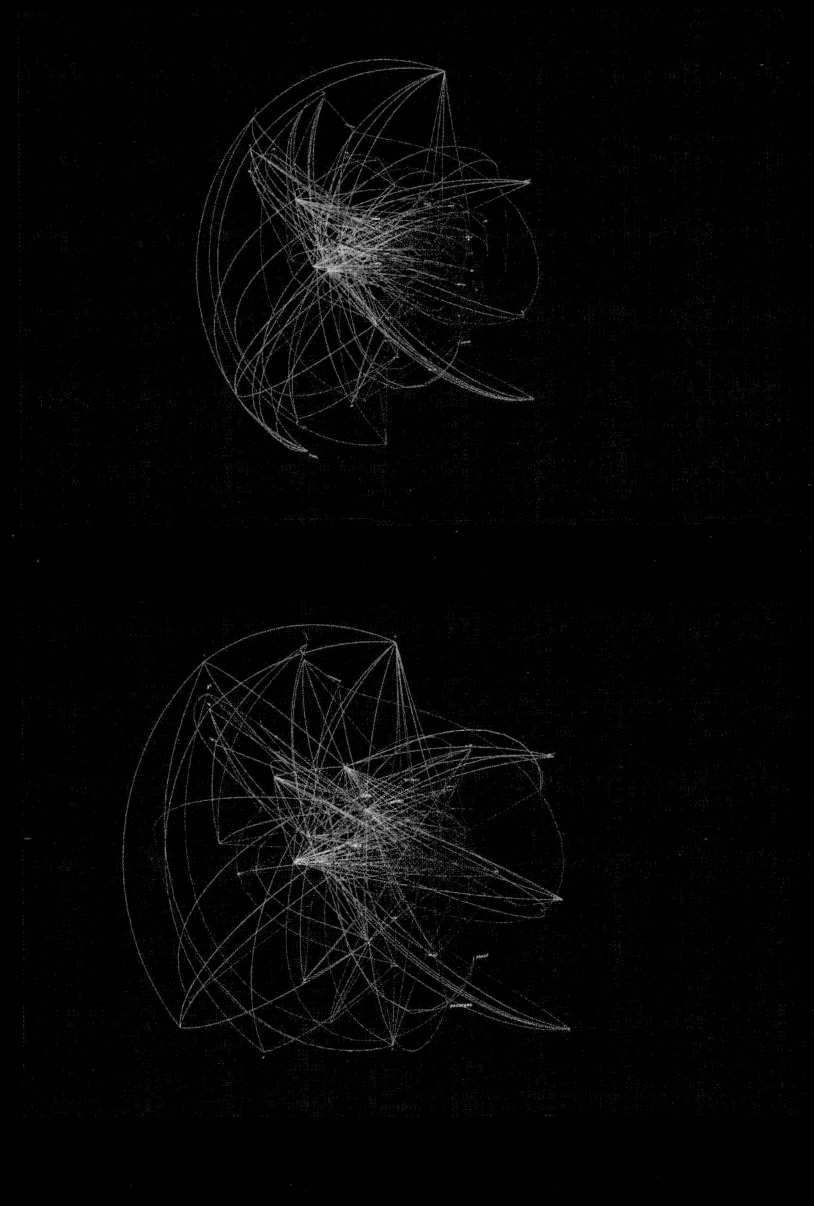

P105 ˝影视实验˝

在 1998 年秋，本杰明做了几个处理影视输入的实验，每个实验是以实际时间进行，以摄象机或电视信号作为输入。
该画面将形象的象数按色调、饱和度、明暗色彩模型重新组织到它们相应的位置。

P105 "Video Experiments"

During the Fall of 1998, Ben did several experiments dealing with video input. Each of these run real-time, using a video camera or television signal as input.
This piece reorganizes the pixels of the image into their respective locations in the hue, saturation, value color model.

P106-107 在这里展示的应用程序根据明亮度来排列形象的色彩，左边颜色较暗，右边较亮。

P106-107 The application shown here arranges each of the individual colors in the image based on their brightness, darker colors at the left and brighter ones to the right.

P108-109 最后的例子是在字体中构成形象，单个字体基于形象区域的明亮度而被选择，这样暗的区域可用小写字体，明亮部分用大写字体，如 ˝W˝。

P108-109 The final example constructs the image out of letters. The individual letters are chosen based on the brightness of that area of the image, so dark areas might use a small lowercase letter, whereas brighter portions use denser letters, such as a W.

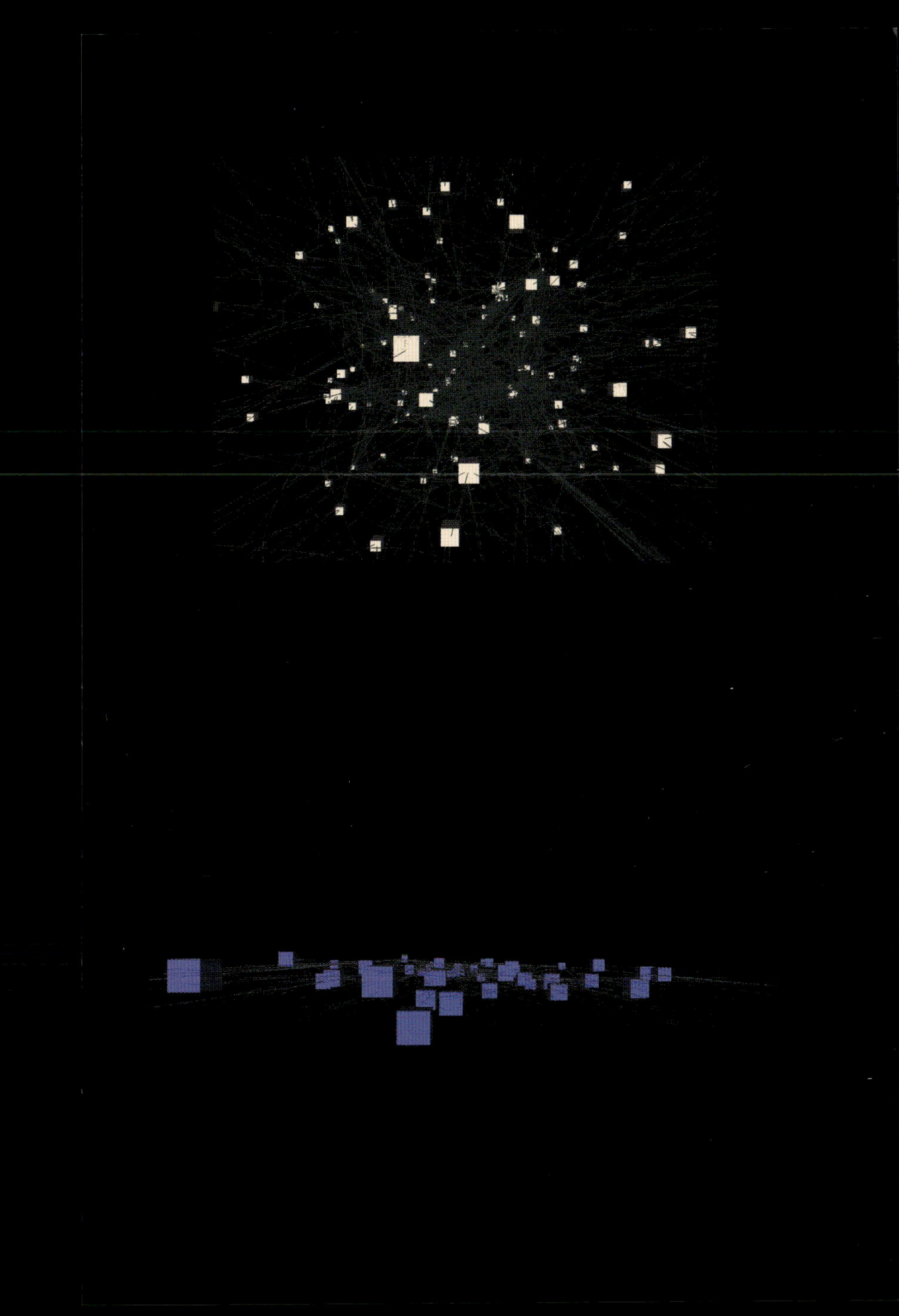

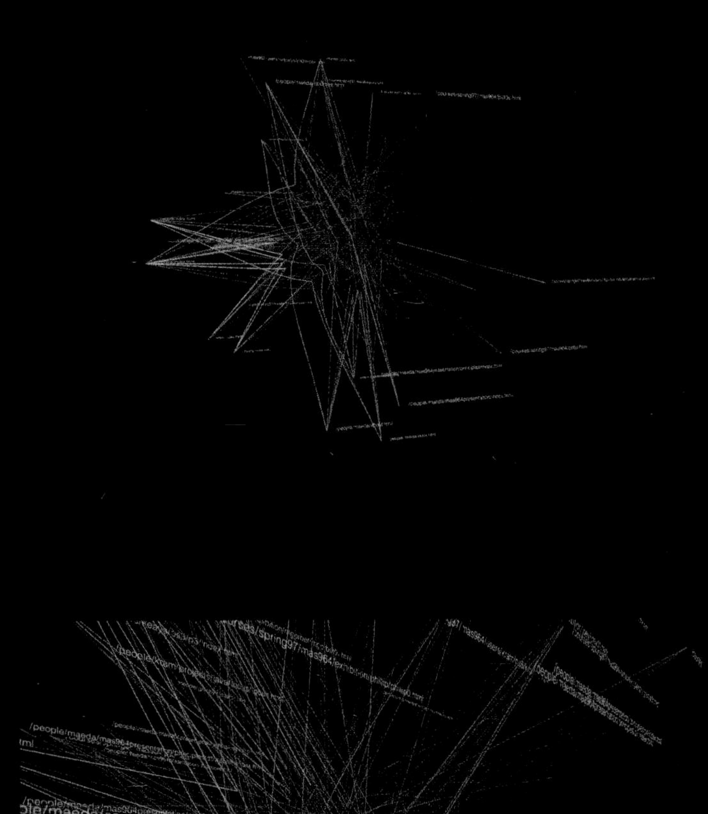
/people/maeda/mas964presentation/principles/index.html
ple/maeda/courses.html
/courses/spring97/mas964/ps9.html
ople/maeda/about.html

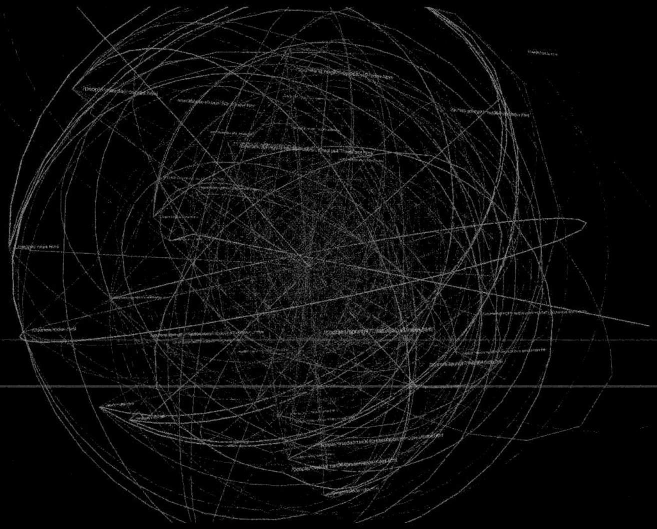

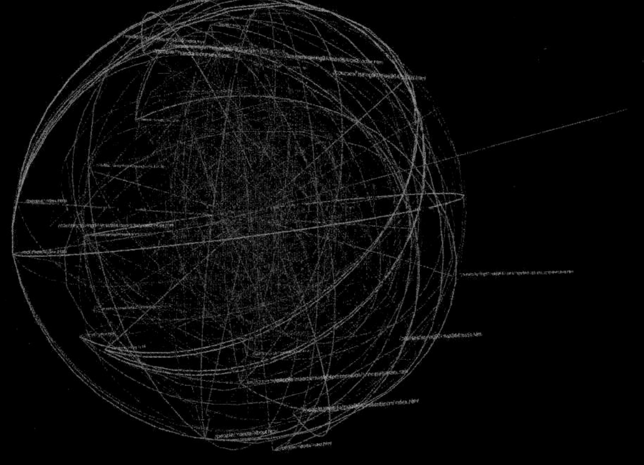

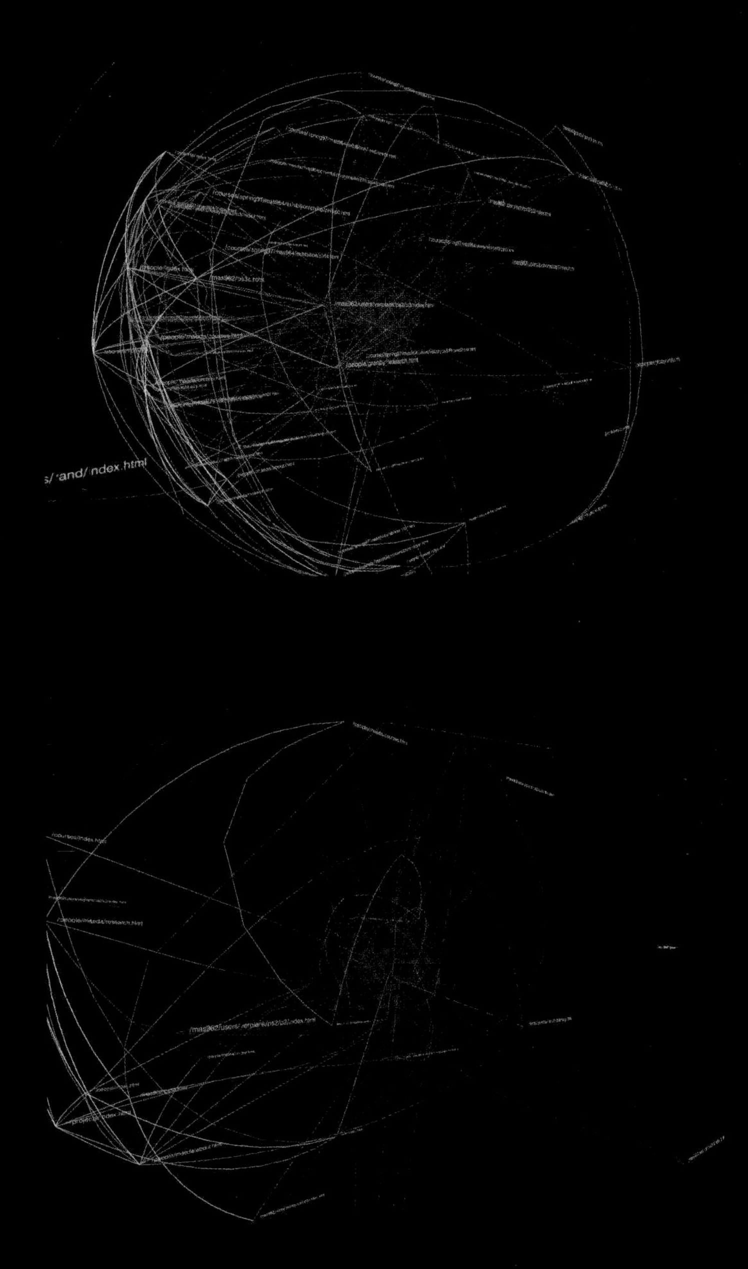
s/ and/ index.html
/mas962/users/ verplank/ps2/p2/index.html
/people/mateda/research.html
/courses/index.html
/projects/index.html

courses
presentation

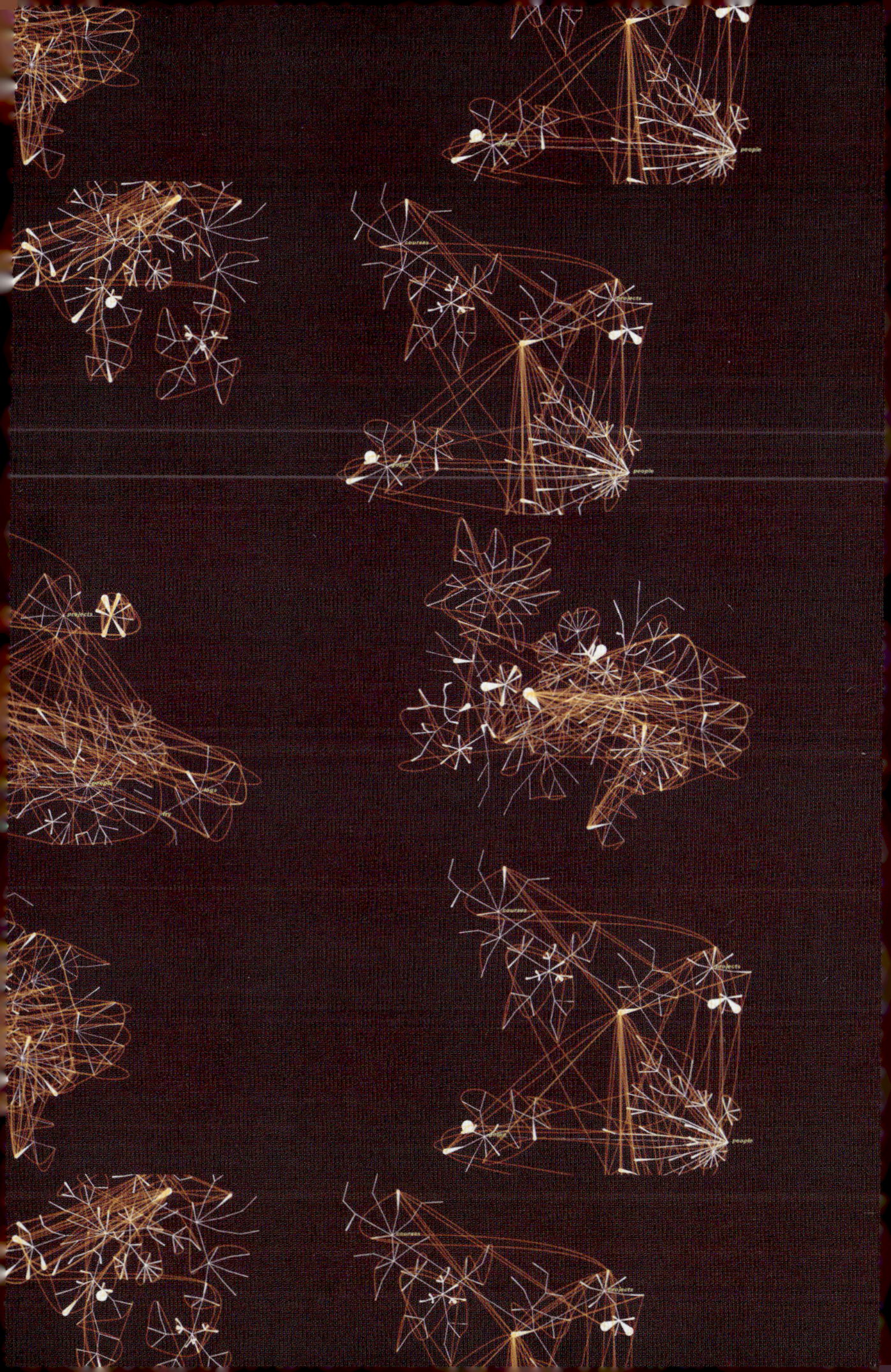
courses
projects
people

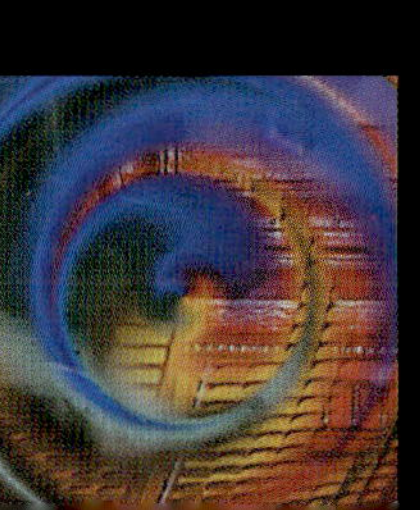

P110-112 "VALENCE"

该项目是采用有机信息视觉化属性来取得更显著的展现。在由马克·吐温著的《THE INNOCENTS ABROAD》一书中的每个特定文字变成了结点，分支用以连结文字，这些文字在文章中是一个个相邻的。一套规则根据有机属性被采用。

P110-112 "Valence"

It is a project that uses the properties of organic information visualization in an attempt to achieve a more telling representation. Every unique word in the book "The Innocents Abroad" by Mark Twain becomes a node. Branches are assigned to connect words that are found adjacent one another in the text. A set of rules is applied, based on the properties of organisms.

P114-119 早期的 VALENCE 版本

P114-119 Earlier versions of Valence

P120-121 "银莲花项目"

该项目是使用"有机信息设计"程序使与绘制网站有联系的问题更加显而易见。来自 ACG 网站的数据在此作为输入。增长的规则可主导网站内新的分支结构的创造。萎缩规则使不用的区域失去影响力，最后移开它们。

单个网页可引起注意力，因为它们比其它的网页更快地被点击，一套主导运动的规则可将相关的区域组合起来。

P120-121 "Anemone"

Anemone is a project that uses the process of Organic Information Design to make this set of problems associated with mapping a web site more approachable. Data from the Aesthetics and Computation Group's web site was used as input in the examples shown here. Rules for growth can govern the creation of new branches of structure within the site. Atrophy rules decay unused areas, eventually removing them.

Individual web pages can call attention to themselves as they are visited more rapidly than others. A set of rules governing movement can group related areas.

## 马克斯·凡·克里克

马克斯·凡·克里克是麻省理工学院电脑科学专业毕业生，二零零零年春加入ACG。在来麻省理工学院之前，他在日本东京附近长大，所以仍视日本为自己的家。马克斯目前对为展示抽象电脑概念而设计视觉语言颇感兴趣。他和布莱恩·史密斯及塔拉·沙克为HICSS-32合著论文。他还是太阳微系统研究室UI设计专利的连署人。

Max Van Kleek is a Computer Science undergraduate at MIT, and joined ACG in Spring 2000. Prior to coming to MIT, he grew up near Tokyo, Japan, which he still considers his home. Max is currently interested in designing visual languages for illustrating abstract computational ideas. He coauthored a paper for HICSS-32 with Brian K. Smith and Tara R. Shankar, and is a cosigner on a UI design patent at Sun Microsystems Labs.

法兰

法兰软件包括一个封闭空间线段的均匀坐标，线段在三维空间的一个平面内，并垂直于平面摆动。

当摆动间隔由线的位置所决定，波浪式形状就出现。以持续的系数多次重复这种关系，可把固定的波浪形粉碎成展现运动的复杂纹理。

Fauna

The fauna environment consists of an even grid of closely spaced line segments that lie perpendicular to a plane in three-dimensional space. These line segments are made to oscillate sinusoidally perpendicular to the plane.

When the phase of oscillation is made dependent on the location of the line, wavelike patterns emerge, multiplying this relationship with a constant coefficient shatters the standing wave-like pattern into complex textures that exhibit motion.

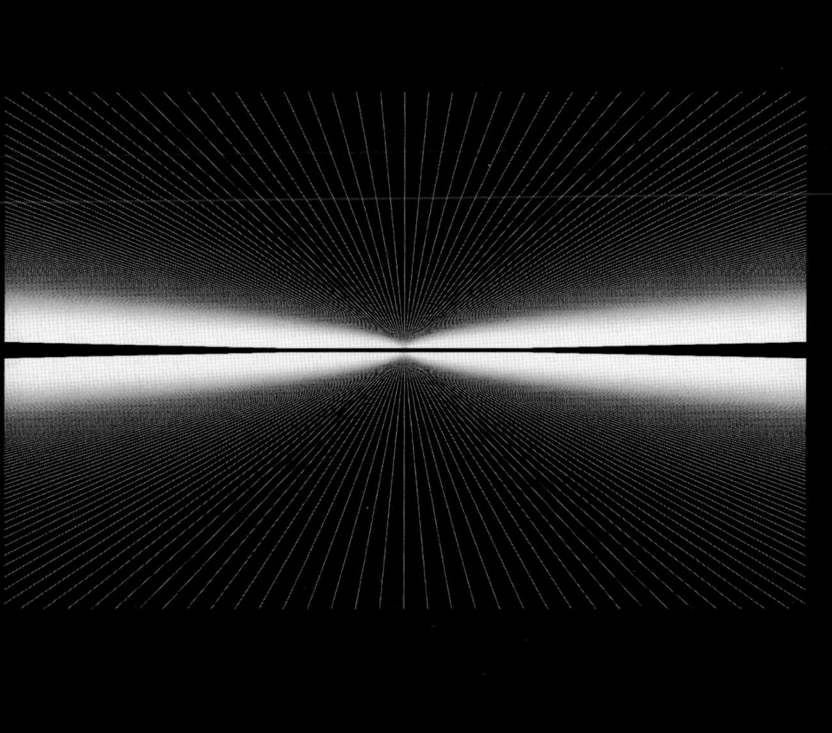

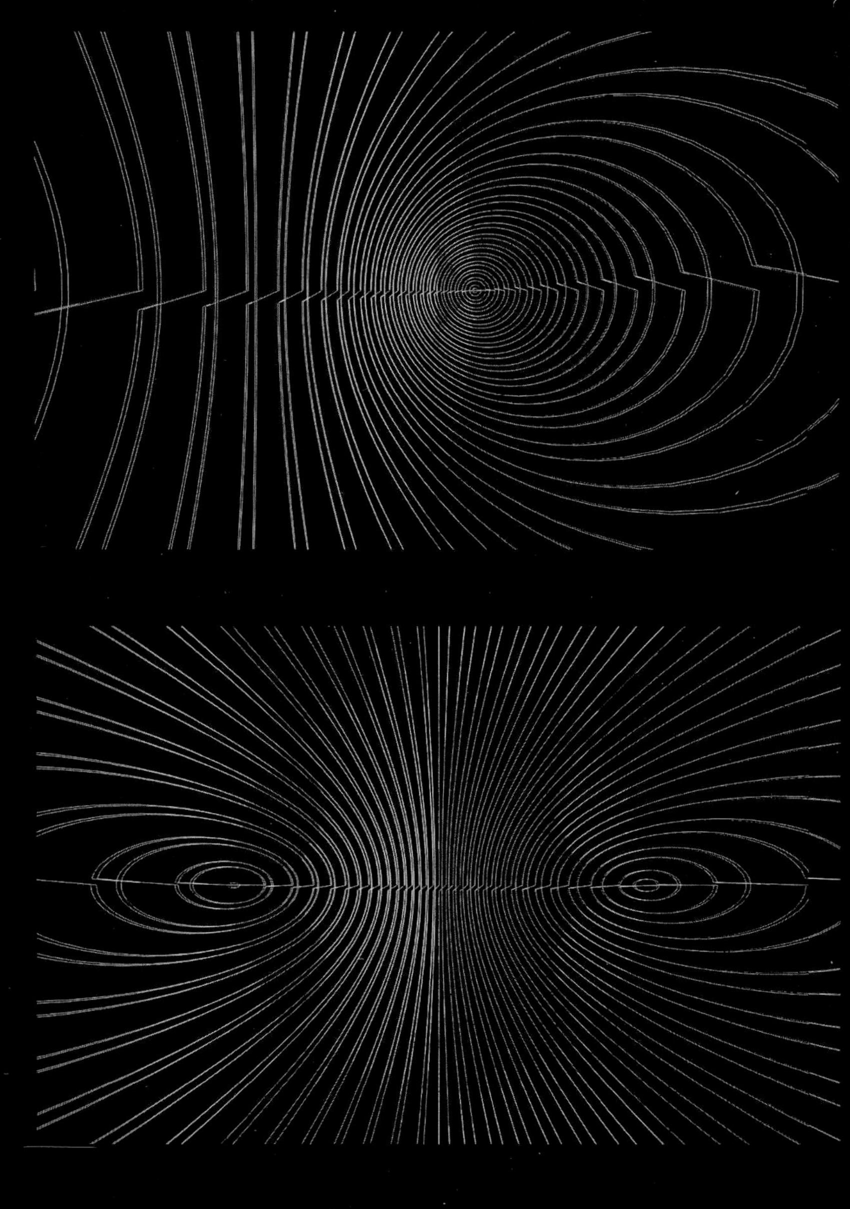